Literature-Based Mini-Lessons

to Teach Writing

★

15 ENGAGING LESSONS THAT HELP
YOUR STUDENTS WRITE HAPPILY EVER AFTER

★

BY SUSAN LUNSFORD

★

SCHOLASTIC
PROFESSIONAL BOOKS

NEW YORK • TORONTO • LONDON • AUCKLAND • SYDNEY
MEXICO CITY • NEW DELHI • HONG KONG

With thanks to my beginning writers

for their constant inspiration

May they always write happily ever after.

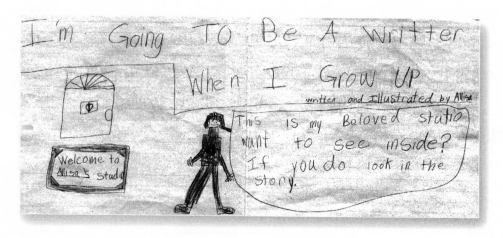

FIRST GRADE AUTHOR

Cover design by Kathy Massaro
Interior Design by Kathy Massaro

ISBN 0-59043372-5

Contents

Acknowledgments

I'm delighted that you've opened this book, that you're committed to helping children develop a love of writing, and that you're interested in introducing children to quality children's literature. I hope you're inspired in some way by the ideas in the book. But before you begin *Literature-Based Mini-Lessons to Teach Writing*, allow me to acknowledge some people who helped me throughout the process of writing it.

To my husband, Brad, who deserves thanks for his constant support and encouragement: For those times when I was "under a writer's spell" in front of my computer, I am thankful that my coffee cup was always magically filled and that you were always willing to listen to "just one more idea..."

To Dan Hade and Judy Fueyo at Penn State, who offered their support during the idea- forming stages; to Bill Teale at *Language Arts,* for originally publishing my article based upon the ideas in this book; and to Wendy Murray at Scholastic, for providing me with the opportunity to share my ideas with other teachers: I offer my heartfelt thanks.

Thanks to the staff at Ferguson Township Elementary School— especially to Cindy Cowan, Jo Dreibelbis, Susan Feldman, and Marge Sutherland— for your words of encouragement and your support in trying new ideas.

Special thanks to the beginning writers who have learned with me. Thank you for sharing your ideas, your stories, and your love of writing.

Finally, to the authors of children's literature. Thank you for your words that paint pictures, words that help us remember, and words that we will never forget. Thank you for giving inspiration to beginning writers and teachers alike.

Portions of this book were first published in the January 1997 issue of *Language Arts,* Volume 74, Number 1.

Author's Note

I've been teaching a multiage classroom of first and second graders for nearly eight years. Recently, I began "looping" my first graders into second grade, keeping the same students for two years in a row. I've been able to watch them develop over a two-year period into readers and writers. When I taught only first graders, I'd have doubted that many of the writing goals in this book would be appropriate for beginning writers—particularly first-grade writers. Now, after putting these lessons and goals into practice, and as I begin a new year with my second graders, who a year ago were first graders in my classroom, I am thrilled by their accomplishments and encouraged by their enthusiasm for writing.

Just one year ago, as first graders, most of these students were writing one-sentence descriptions under a picture. Many of their phonetically spelled words contained only initial consonant sounds or labels they had copied from the board. Now, as beginning second graders whose fine-motor and phonetic-spelling skills are more developed, they're starting stories with advanced leads, using descriptive language, and writing complete stories from the first day. A few samples of my students' successes demonstrate the effectiveness of literature-based mini-lessons to teach writing.

Brett* began first grade as a very hesitant writer. He needed much reassurance and assistance to begin a writing task. By October he was showing more confidence and would retell his stories without matching his words to the print. Much of what he wrote was still unreadable by others.

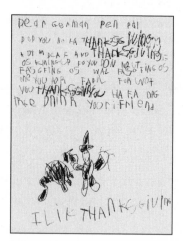

Brett, November, Grade 1

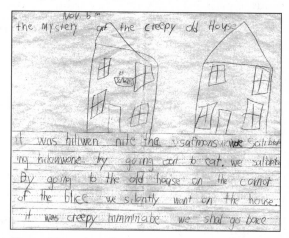

Brett, November, Grade 2

As a second grader, Brett is composing complete stories that are more easily deciphered. He shows great confidence and pride in his writing, which contains descriptive language and a style he has borrowed from the experts.

It was Halloween night. The Safmons were celebrating Halloween by going out to eat. We celebrated by going to the old house on the corner of the block. We silently went in the house. It was creepy. "M-m-m-m—maybe we should go back ..."

---

* The names of all students have been changed so that they may remain anonymous.

Meghan began first grade as a confident, enthusiastic, but slow-paced writer. She worked hard to get the sounds "just right," often losing "great ideas" since her fingers were unable to keep up with her thoughts. She spent much of her writing time rereading what she had written, trying to remember her original idea. Her stories, although usually complete, consisted of simple sentence patterns with extra details that she explained orally.

Meghan, November, Grade 1
"Shorty the Giraffe"

Shorty was a giraffe. She was a nice little giraffe. She lived in a jungle with her mommy. They lived by a little tree. They liked it ...

As a second grader, Meghan can write complex sentences. She takes her story writing seriously and often appears to be "under a writer's spell," searching for the words to make her idea sound "just right." Meghan's writing style began to emerge once her fingers caught up with her thinking.

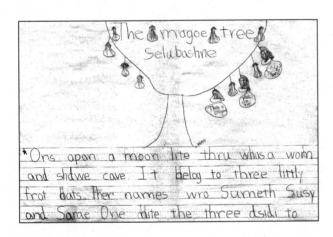

Meghan, October, Grade 2
"The Mango Tree Celebration"

Once upon a moonlit night there was a warm and shadowy cave. It belonged to three little fruit bats. Their names were Samantha, Susy, and Sarah. One night the three decided to go for a fly. As soon as they spotted a mango tree, an owl flew out from the trees and screeched at them. The smallest, Susy, stayed very far away. Finally the owl gave up. The bats celebrated at the mango tree. The owl found a new home and they all lived happily ever after. The End.

Perhaps most encouraging is Matthew. At the beginning of first grade, his stories were told through pictures and one-sentence descriptions that were often unreadable. Writing wasn't easy for Matthew. He labored over matching letters with sounds. Still, his ideas were creative, and his oral language ability was strong. He loved read-aloud time and had excellent memory for details of the stories.

Matthew, November, Grade 1

I didn't have any milk.

At the beginning of second grade, Matthew is writing complete stories with descriptive language and feeling confident. He has become a successful writer.

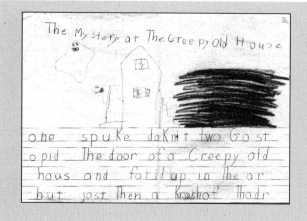

Matthew, November, Grade 2

One spooky dark night two ghosts opened the door of a creepy old house and floated up in the air. But just then a crash of thunder shook the earth. Two streaks of lightning shot the earth. I whispered to my brother, "Did you see that? Two little white sacks were floating in the air." Before I could say a word, a creepy old house caught my eye. I screamed. My brother asked me, "What is the matter?" I told him what I saw. Steven, my brother, looked out the window. He saw the haunted house. Steven and me tiptoed outside on the cold slippy red stairs. We slid down the hard rocky driveway and finally Steven and me reached the creepy old house. Taking our flashlights out of our pockets, we crept up the old stairs and heard some music. We opened the door that it was coming from. And in the room, our mom and dad made a surprise birthday party.
The End.

Without exception, these writers made notable progress in our writers' workshop environment. Most encouraging, they eagerly anticipate writers' workshop time. I overheard one returning second grader tell a first grader, "Wait until we start writers' workshop—it's the best!" As these "expert" second-grade writers began another year of literature-based mini-lessons in writing, I was shown again that the mini-lessons I'd once thought might be too advanced for their abilities were actually just right.

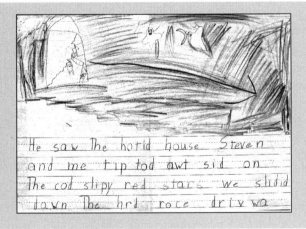

Introduction

One day during writers' workshop, Emily raised her hand. She was trying to draw a picture of a puppy sitting on her doorstep. The holes worn through her paper by her eraser told me she had attempted this task many times before. "Can you draw me a puppy, please?" she asked with the voice of a very frustrated first grader. "I could, but then it would be my picture," I said, "and I know you want this to be yours. Let's look at the book *Best Friends* by Steven Kellogg. He's the expert on drawing puppies." We opened the book to the picture of the puppy on the step, and Emily's face relaxed. Seeing how an "expert" had successfully tackled a similar problem seemed to make Emily feel better. She seemed less threatened by the task, as if she knew she'd succeed. When she finished, her dog didn't look like Steven Kellogg's, but it was a vast improvement over previous attempts.

One young writer gets help from the "experts."

For several years, I had used children's literature to help my students become more confident illustrators but blundered through writers' workshop mini-lessons. I knew from 11 years as a primary teacher that the best writers' workshop mini-lessons evolve from students' writing, but I still wasn't sure how to design lessons that would best meet the needs of beginning writers. What feat of magic could I perform in a 10–20 minute mini-lesson that would improve students' writing techniques and encourage them to write more? When I saw Emily's success that day, it struck me that the authors of children's literature, the real writing "experts," might provide the magic I needed to bring to our mini-lessons.

Nancie Atwell credits Lucy Calkins with the concept of mini-lesson and defines it as:

> *a brief meeting that begins the workshop where the whole class addresses an issue that's arisen in previous workshops or in pieces of students' writing. The point of the mini-lesson is to expose students to ideas and information that will be reinforced in individual conferences through the rest of the school year.*

> —*In the Middle: Writing, Reading, and Learning With Adolescents*
> by Nancie Atwell (Heinemann, 1987)

Reading stories aloud on a daily basis familiarizes children with a wealth of books you'll have at your disposal for literature-based mini-lessons.

A mini-lesson is also an opportunity to share personal knowledge about writing. Atwell wrote that "the problems students come up against mirror problems I confront in my own writing. These are professional writers' problems, too." She claims her favorite mini-lessons are those in which she shares tricks of the trade with her students.

In my own teaching, my best lessons come from the authors of children's literature. Through student conferences, group sharing times, and discoveries in literature, I identify the problems that need focused instruction. For example, we explore questions such as: How do the experts start a story? What kind of exciting words do they use to make their stories enjoyable? What do the experts include to make their stories complete? These questions become the topics of mini-lessons over the course of one school year. As each new topic arises, I search my favorite works of children's literature for examples of how published authors handled each area. Even beginning writers agree that the "hot chocolate as thick and rich as melted chocolate bars" that Chris Van Allsburg describes in *The Polar Express* sounds more exciting than "good hot chocolate." Similarly, most young writers are impressed by Jon Scieszka's twist on a "once upon a time" story in *The Frog Prince Continued*: "Well, let's just say they lived sort of happily for a long time." And students become indignant at the thought of Maurice Sendak leaving Max in his room "without eating anything" and never getting to visit the forest in *Where the Wild Things Are*. By bringing examples of literature such as these to a mini-lesson and focusing instruction on the features of excellent writing, I hoped my students would try similar alternatives and techniques in their own writing. But perhaps even more important, I hoped to heighten students' awareness of quality literature and to help them view literature with a writer's eye.

In discerning what motivated my students and which literature provides the best models for writers' workshop mini-lesson, I discovered that my own enthusiasm for certain types of literature has the greatest impact. For example, when I introduce *The Polar Express* during read-aloud time, I comment that Chris Van Allsburg is one of my favorite authors, because he makes me feel like I am a part of his stories and his words paint pictures in my mind as clearly as his pictures do. I point out a few of my favorite sentences and ask students to add their own feelings.

Through this kind of modeling and discussion of literature, students begin to show enthusiasm for literature by rushing to check out my favorites from the library. Soon they are extending this appreciation to different books. It doesn't take long even for young children to form their own preferences and styles as readers and writers in a learning environment that surrounds them with quality children's literature. I make sure to include time for read-aloud and writing every day. My enthusiasm for children's literature and my love of writing are two qualities I share with every child I teach.

There is a positive connection between the children's enthusiasm for books and their excitement about writers' workshop. I use this excitement to help build confidence, which, over time, I began to see as the most important ingredient for success for my beginning writers. This is not surprising, but for beginning writers there are several kinds of confidence to build—confidence in risk-taking, in sound-spelling connection, in story sharing, and in topic selection. As I developed the literature-based mini-lessons and put them into practice, the atmosphere the students and I built together became one of sharing, learning from each other, and, ultimately, supporting each other's strengths and weaknesses. The authors of children's literature, with all their words of wisdom, humor, and encouragement, are constant reminders of the successes that can be achieved with confidence and effort.

In this book, I'll share some of the literature-based mini-lessons I developed for use in my first- and second-grade multiage classroom. The writing abilities of the group range from the very beginning writer who uses one-letter representations for words or pictures and provides oral interpretations, to the very competent writer who has a developed literary style with complex sentences. All of my young writers benefit from the same literature-based mini-lessons in writing, along with the individualized conferences I provide them.

I hope the ideas in this book give you greater confidence in planning writers' workshop mini-lessons that focus on the features of excellent writing. I'm sure your students will feel a sense of relief knowing that they can turn to the "experts" when faced with a problem in writing. The authors of children's literature are always there, ready to lend a hand, to make teachers and children alike feel more successful in their daily journeys as writers.

What a Literature-Based Writers' Workshop Looks Like

CHAPTER 1

A long with figuring out what kinds of lessons make the most effective writers' workshop, it's important to discover how a writers' workshop should be set up. The arrangement of the classroom, the daily schedule, and the organization of student work were elements I focused on for several years before I was sure what worked best for me. Following is a description of what I decided is an effective writers' workshop for my classroom. I hope some of my discoveries will help you in arranging a writers' workshop environment that suits you and your students.

The Classroom

QUIET ZONE VERSUS SILENT ZONE

As we begin working in our writers' workshop, I designate specific areas of the classroom for certain clearly defined purposes. Since my classroom is centered upon cooperative learning experiences, I've found that tables or desks clustered together are most functional for the student work area. Typically, I have five groups of four to five children placed in the center of my classroom. During writers' workshop, this area is known as **The Quiet Zone** and is designed for those writers who require a quiet environment to accomplish any writing task. Whispering is permitted as it relates to writing.

There are times when some students, who may be "under a writer's spell," need absolute quiet. A table

Authors working in The Quiet Zone

with four chairs located in a corner of the room becomes known as **The Silent Zone—Please Do Not Disturb**. Students who sit there do not want to be interrupted for any reason.

The Conference Area is where I meet with students to talk about their writing. My anecdotal notebooks, pencils, erasers, and student recording sheets are placed here along with the box of stories "For Mrs. L." Having materials and a clearly defined work space helps me to make the best use of conference time with students.

SHARING CORNERS AND CENTERS

I label two corners of the classroom as **Sharing Corners**. A pair of students may work quietly in one of these corners to edit or simply share written work. Students also occasionally work together to write a story. Having an area designated for sharing keeps interruptions of others working nearby to a minimum.

Two young authors work in a Sharing Corner

I also organize two centers to make many writing-related items readily available to students. **The Writing Center** includes necessary supplies such as sharpened pencils, a stapler, paper clips, erasers, crayons, sticky notes, and various kinds of paper. A chart labeled "Good Writers..." hangs on the wall nearby to remind my writers to plan ahead, use lots of exciting words, and to take time to reread their finished stories.

This center allows for more productive writing time, since children don't waste time sharpening pencils or locating lost erasers. It also facilitates independence and a sense of ownership of the classroom.

The Favorite Books Box is an important place for writers with a particular problem. This is where the books we deem our "favorites"—or those we may share for a particular

Good Writers...

**plan ahead.

**start with an exciting beginning.

**have stories with a beginning, a middle, and an end.

**don't stop in the middle of their story.

**make sense when they write.

**use lots of exciting words.

**take time for careful illustrations.

**take time to check their story when they are finished.

Are you a **good** writer?

A chart lists the steps a writer follows from idea to publication.

purpose during a mini-lesson—are easily located at a moment's notice. Pages of these books are frequently marked with sticky notes to highlight given sentences or pictures. A student who's having difficulty thinking of a writing topic can frequently be found perusing the box of favorite books to find an idea for his own story. We also keep beginning-level dictionaries, a selection of pictionaries, and a thesaurus at this center, along with student booklets containing weekly word lists. Charts of commonly used words are kept here for easy access when a word should be "book-spelled" rather than "sound-spelled."

Doing research at the "Favorite Books" Box

Our Writers' Workshop Schedule

Our plan for each day is listed on the board as the students arrive. However, this schedule simply shows the order of the day's activities. To help the students become familiar with the writing routine, I list the following writers' workshop schedule on a permanent chart near the writing center. We have writers' workshop for one hour four times a week.

Writers' Workshop Schedule

Writers' Meeting
15 minutes

Writing Time
30 minutes
(The first 5 minutes must be silent)

Sharing Time
15 minutes

The "writers' meeting" is the term I use with my students for our mini-lesson. These mini-lessons, which are whole class, motivate students to become real writers by bolstering their confidence in their abilities. Following the day's mini-lesson, I

pass out the children's writing folders, which we keep in a box next to the mini-lesson area. After a final comment to wrap up our writers' meeting, I announce that it is writing time.

At the beginning of the year, writing time is a period of 15–20 minutes. I lengthen it as the students become more focused writers and as their attention spans increase. I find it helpful to insist that the first five minutes of writing time be silent. We define silent as "no talking to others or raising hands for assistance," but, of course, there is always the buzz of sounding out words in a classroom full of young writers. This silent time allows the students to become focused on their stories and provides a better atmosphere for organizing thoughts. Beginning with a silent writing time naturally leads to a quieter writers' workshop all-in-all because the noise level tends to remain low. I never announce when silent writing time is over but begin circulating around the room after the five-minute period.

I use silent writing time to model my own writing for the students—either in my writing journal or using an overhead projector. Modeling demonstrates practical uses of writing. I may write a story, a letter to family or a friend, or reflections about an effective mini-lesson. More important, what I write during silent writing time often becomes the basis for a future mini-lesson. During the early part of the school year, I make a point of using my writing to establish an atmosphere of trust and to model story sharing.

Sharing Stories

Sharing stories is an integral part of a complete writers' workshop and should not be overlooked because of the time constraints of the school day. Sharing work and receiving feedback from an audience is a valuable part of the writing process. It shows students that writers write to communicate with others and provides them with a concrete audience. Sharing is particularly crucial for beginning writers, who benefit from expanding their often egocentric viewpoints. Listening to the ideas of others also helps young writers develop their own writing style by giving students the chance to form opinions about what makes a particular story more enjoyable or not so enjoyable. When students know they will be given an opportunity each day to share what they've written, they're more likely to put greater effort into each day's work—to do their best.

Because I know teachers have a limited amount of time for sharing stories, I've developed several ways to fit it in effectively. At the beginning of the year, we share as a whole group. First, I model my own writing, posing questions such as "What did you like about my story?" or "What would you change in my story?" The students also share their stories in pairs at the Sharing Corners. Once a comfortable atmosphere for sharing has been established, the students share their stories in a small group. This is especially effective when the stack of finished stories piles up. A member of each of five groups can share stories at the same time. The downside to sharing in a smaller group setting is that children receive feedback from only a few fellow writers.

Another effective way for students to share their stories is in one of two sharing circles. I divide the class in half, making sure to include a range of writing abilities in each group. I ask the students to form a circle with their group, usually at opposite ends of the room to minimize interruptions. A parent helper may assist one group while I work with the other.

Sharing Time

Parent Helpers

Although a writers' workshop can operate with the teacher alone, I've found parent helpers to be an important key to my success, and I try to have one parent volunteer for each writers' workshop. The parent's main responsibilities are to assist students when they're having problems with sound-spelling and when they 're "stuck" with a particular part of a story. This help allows me time to have uninterrupted individual student conferences, which are particularly important for early writers who need lots of confidence-boosting, reassurance, and assistance with sounding out words. I want to point out that I do not begin conferences until after the five minutes of silent writing and until after I have circulated around the room several times and am satisfied that all students are sure of their writing topics and goals for the day's workshop.

Organizing Student Work

An interruption that can easily be handled as a housekeeping chore is the all-too-frequently asked, "I'm done with my story. Where do I put it?" or "I'm done with my story. Now what do I do?" I address the latter question by simply saying "It's still writing time. You may either start a new story or share your finished story with a friend."

Two labeled boxes have eliminated the first question. One is labeled "Stories to Share" and is kept near an "author's chair." After each writer's workshop sharing time, any stories not yet shared may be placed in this box. (If I am using two

writer's sharing circles as mentioned previously, I place a separate box beside each of two author's chairs.) Throughout the remainder of that day, we use otherwise wasted minutes (for example, while we're waiting for a special visitor or for the end-of-the-day announcements to be made) to have an author read a story to the rest of the class. We get extra, much-needed sharing time, and the stories are readily available for sharing.

A second box, labeled "To Mrs.L.," is kept on the table where I hold my student conferences. Children place their stories in this box if they are finished and they wish to share them with me prior to sharing them in a sharing circle or if they need help with a particular problem. A student may place a sticky note on a particular story with the words "I'm stuck." I try to hold a conference with these writers first during writing time. An author who wants his or her story displayed in the hallway or "published" may label it as such with a sticky note and place it in the box so that the student and I can read it together and be sure it's ready.

The keys to organizing an effective writers' workshop are simplicity and flexibility. When I first began the workshop system, I had four boxes with various labels. This was more confusing than helpful. I tried to conduct student conferences while kneeling beside children at their work area. Besides being uncomfortable, I was continually interrupted by other writers at the table and found it difficult to concentrate on the conference. You'll need to experiment until you find a system to accommodate your style of teaching and your students' needs.

Conference Time: Mrs. L. works with a student, while Mrs. Y. helps those in The Quiet Zone

Getting the Workshop Started

CHAPTER 2

The Mini-Lessons

The Writing Goals

The Mini-Lessons	The Writing Goals
"What If?"	To explore ideas for writing
Everyone Is an Expert at Something	To view selves as writers
Where Else Do Ideas Come From?	To explore story inspirations
Sharing Stories	To share stories with an audience

Favorite Books to Use

Books about being a writer, such as:

Arthur Writes a Story by Marc Brown

Aunt Isabel Tells a Good One by Kate Duke

If You Were a Writer by Joan Lowery Nixon

Books based on real events, such as:

The Art Lesson by Tomie dePaola

My Rotten Redheaded Older Brother by Patricia Polacco

The Painter by Peter Catalanotto

Those Summers by Aliki

"What If?"

GOAL To explore ideas for writing

Coming up with an idea for writing is the first obstacle many young writers must tackle. To be motivating, the idea must originate with the child, not be given by the teacher. In anticipation of the dreaded "I don't know what to write" raised by many a beginning writer, I address this issue early in the school year. I let my students know that all writers face this dilemma but that if authors let this problem beat them, there would be no stories. Writers, young and experienced, must be constantly looking for ideas, be confident, and imagine what if...

A typical "What if" mini-lesson goes something like this:

Mrs. L.: Yesterday we read the book, *If You Were a Writer* by Joan Lowery Nixon. She reminded me of a problem all writers sometimes face— the "I-don't-know-what-to-write" problem. Let's try to remember some of her suggestions so that when we find ourselves asking "What should I write," we have some places to look for ideas. I remember Joan Lowery Nixon wrote that "if you were a writer, you would search for ideas. Ideas are everywhere. The more you look for ideas, the more you will find."

Meghan: Yes, she said you need to "let ideas bounce in your brain, and poke them, and pinch them."

Mrs. L.: What a clever way to think about ideas. I think that's true. And since we are all writers but never know when an idea might jump into our minds, we need to be writing detectives, constantly looking for ideas. Today I thought we would be writing detectives answering the question, "What if?" Remember what happened when Melia said "What if?" in *If You Were a Writer*?

Ben: Oh, a dog ran down the street being chased by a boy. She wondered, What if a necklace with diamonds was caught on the dog's collar?

Mrs. L.: Great! Let me find that page. Melia imagined: "What if the necklace has been stolen by a pirate? What if the boy is really a detective in disguise? What would happen then?" That could make a good idea for a story.

Matthew: Yes, I'm going to write a story about that.

Mrs. L.: I can't wait to see how it turns out.

Amanda: I liked the "what if a bear stole the honey jar from inside their house?" Remember Melia's mother couldn't find the honey in the cupboard. Last night my little brother couldn't find his favorite teddy bear. Maybe a real bear snuck into our house and took it!

Mrs. L.:   That could make an interesting story too. "What if a real bear stole my teddy bear ..."

Let's see if we can think of some more "what if's" of our own. Think of something that has happened to you. Then we'll ask "What if?," and I'll write the ideas on this chart.

Brett: Well, this morning when I was waiting at the bus stop, my friend's dog tried to get on the bus and go to school.

Mrs. L.:   What if a dog came to school for the day? I think that would be a fun story to write. I know my dog would love to come to school with me! What other ideas do you have for a "what if " story?

Alissa: What if I were reading a story about a dinosaur and the dinosaur hopped out of the book?

Mrs. L: That's a great idea, and the character from just about any book could hop into the room and help us write an exciting story.

Tell me another idea for a story.

Ben: My mom says there are dust bunnies that tickle little children who hide under the bed.

Mrs. L.:   Great idea! What if the tickling dust bunnies were hungry for peanut butter and jelly sandwiches and kept tickling the little boy until the babysitter brought them a peanut butter sandwich with extra jelly?

Lauren: Oh, please write that story, Mrs. Lunsford!

Mrs. L.:   The dust bunny story does sound like fun to write. Any of us could write a story using this same "what if" and all the stories would be different. Let's add this idea to our chart of "what if's."

Brett: That gives me another idea. But this one is about a monster hiding under the bed. What if it was a book-eating monster who decided to go to the library to eat all the books?

Matthew: I think we could think of "what if's" all day long ...

Mrs. L.:   I think you're right! Let's try to write some "what if" stories using these ideas or others you may think of.

What if...

- my dog got on the school bus and went to school?
- a dinosaur jumped off the page of the book I was reading?
- tickling dust bunnies were hiding under the bed?
- my cat climbed up a tree and was saved by the tooth fairy?
- I found a baby dinosaur in the woods and it began to talk to me?
- a shark could walk on land?

This lesson allows for a natural discussion of stories that students have ended too soon. During sharing time that day, many first graders shared beginning "what if's." Colleen wrote: "What if a cat turned into a rat and stayed into a rat. And then what happened is another cat turned into a rat. The end." She used excellent sound-spelling, but her audience told her she couldn't end the story yet. They asked her to tell more about what happened to the cat-rat. So she added: "A rat turned into a cat and another rat turned into a cat and they were friends happily ever after. The end." Her audience was satisfied at having the friends living happily ever after.

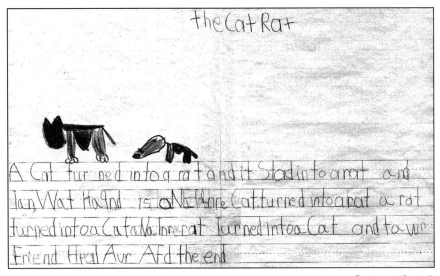

Colleen, Age 6

Extending the Mini-Lesson

HELPFUL IDEA SHEET

Whenever a student has an idea for a "what if" story, the student jots it down on a sheet of paper labeled "What If's," which is stapled to the inside cover of his writing folder. This assures that the ideas are readily available if the student is at a loss for a writing topic during writing time. Occasionally we take a few minutes of writing time or time during a mini-lesson to share a few new "what if" ideas. Students keep adding ideas and, before we know it, we've created many more writing topics.

GAME

"What if?" turns into a kind of game for my students whenever we have a few minutes to share. We begin by having someone name an object or person—for example, "brother." Another student names an object or a place, maybe a "skateboard." Given these initial ideas, we brainstorm possible "what if's," such as "What if my brother's skateboard grew wings and flew him to the moon…" or "What if my brother's skateboard took him on a journey back in time…or into the future …"

THE SILENT ZONE

On another day, I reread the beginning of *If You Were a Writer* where Melia talks about her mother being "under a writer's spell" or of "thinking of what to write next." This is a great way to introduce **The Silent Zone** where no talking is allowed

(see Chapter 1). I explain that when a writer feels like he is under a spell, it is almost as if the pencil moves like magic, because ideas keep flowing. This writer needs a place where he will not be interrupted for any reason. By talking about this spell-like feeling that Melia's mother and all writers experience, students can develop a sensitivity to others and to their different needs as writers.

MEET THE AUTHORS

At read-aloud time, I frequently ask children to think of where the author's story idea may have originated. This helps to increase students' awareness of possible outlets for ideas and helps them view literature with a writer's eye.

In *Meet the Authors and Illustrators* (Volumes One and Two), authors use examples of their published works to tell about their thinking processes while writing. "There are wonderful ideas for stories all around," says Marc Brown (Volume 2, p. 16). "All you have to do is keep your eyes and your ears open. It might be something that happens at home with your sister. It might happen in your classroom. It might be on the bus." These books are an excellent way to begin a mini-lesson on story ideas and to give beginning writers a chance to "meet" the authors and illustrators of their favorite books.

STUDENT PROGRESS

Dinosaur "What-If's"

While doing a unit on dinosaurs, our "what-if" stories were filled with this prehistoric life theme.

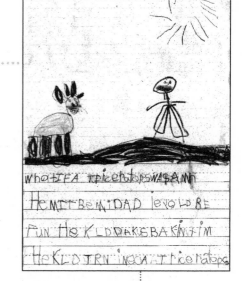

FIRST-GRADE AUTHOR:

What if a Triceratops was around... ▶

FIRST-GRADE AUTHOR:

One day I went to bed and when I woke up I was back in the Cretaceous Period...

FIRST-GRADE AUTHOR:

One day I was reading a dinosaur book and all of the sudden it started chasing me all around the house...

▼

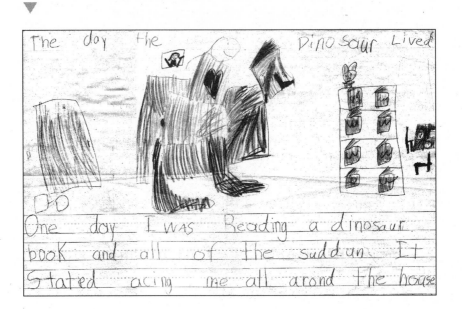

Writing "what if" stories

Everyone Is an Expert at Something

GOAL To view selves as writers

*A*t the beginning of first grade, students often look at writing as something that only real authors or adults do. I frequently hear at least one of my first graders exclaim with fear in his voice, "But, I can't write," when I announce the year's first writing task. By second grade and often the end of first grade, children are convinced that what they write can usually be read by others and themselves and believe they have a story worth telling. The sooner I am able to help my students view themselves as writers, the sooner they become active participants during writers' workshop and, therefore, make greater progress. I often begin this confidence-building by proving that everyone is an expert at something and that there are some stories that only certain individuals can tell.

In preparation for this lesson, I chart five personal experiences that are potential story topics:

Good Story Topics

- The first time I went on a roller coaster
- Sydney's first puppy class
- The night my family was stranded in a snowstorm
- The day before Christmas when I broke my foot
- Hiking in the woods and spotting a bear

Mrs. L: I have been thinking about where I get ideas for my stories. I realized that most of the stories I write are based on things that have happened to me. I am the "expert" on writing stories about my experiences. Nobody else can tell how I felt whenever my cat ran away or the first time I went on a roller coaster. Other people have had these experiences too, but as writers, each person would tell the story in a different way.

I charted five things that happened to me—stories that I am an expert at telling.

(We read the list together)

I could choose any of these ideas to write about, and I think they would be stories you'd enjoy hearing. But I have to look at the list carefully to decide which of those stories I feel like writing today. I feel like writing a funny story today, so I think I'll write about Sydney's first puppy class.

Can you think of any experiences you've had recently that make you an expert on writing a certain story?

Ellen: My sister had a birthday party, and she cried when we sang to her.

Mrs. L.: Birthday parties make terrific story ideas, and you are now an expert on birthday parties.

Stevie: I think my trip to Disney World would make a good story. I had fun.

Mrs. L.: Stories about vacations are fun to tell and they help you remember your trip. Now we have a Disney World expert in our class.

Katie: I'm in a dance recital soon. Could I write about that?

Carrie: I would. I have a test at karate class, and I'm writing about that. I'm nervous, and I won't write the ending of the story because I don't know if I passed yet.

Mrs. L.: I think all of these ideas would make great stories. We have many different experts with many different stories to tell. I've chosen some stories written by a few of our favorite authors. The idea for each story came from something that really happened to the author. The author may have added some different parts or changed the story to make it more interesting or exciting.

Remember when we read *Those Summers* by Aliki?

Meghan: Yes, the story is about her trip to the beach when she was a little girl.

Stephanie: She made it look like olden times because of the way she listened to the radio instead of TV—and the bathing caps. We don't have to wear those anymore.

Mrs. L.: What reason do you think Aliki had for wanting to write this story?

Stephanie: I think she wanted to tell us about her vacations with her cousins.

Mrs. L.: I bet you're right, and I think *Those Summers* is the kind of story that makes the reader say, "Oh, I have done that, too." It reminded me of beach trips with my cousins when I was younger. We played checkers on rainy days too. I like when a book makes me think of happy memories. I want to read the book over and over again to remember what those times were like.

Matthew: If she didn't write them down she might forget them.

Mrs. L.: That's a good point. Remembering is a great reason to write a story.

John: Because then you have the story forever.

Mrs. L.: Right. Aliki is an expert on telling beach stories. What do you think makes Patricia Polacco an expert on writing *My Rotten Redheaded Older Brother*?

Kristen: I bet she has a rotten redheaded older brother. I know how she feels because I have a rotten brother too.

Mrs. L.: Oh, really? This story makes those of us with older brothers or sisters think of similar experiences we may have had. I bet Patricia Polacco told this story—about the time she fell off the merry-go-round and had to get stitches—out loud many times. But I wonder when she realized it might make a good story for children to hear and wrote it down.

Brian: Maybe she was telling the story to some children, and they really liked it and told her to write it down.

Mrs. L.: Could be. I guess we should always be looking for good story ideas. Do you think Patricia Polacco remembered everything in her story exactly the way it happened all those years ago?

Dana: No, she may have added things to make it better.

Mrs. L.: Right. I love the real pictures she puts at the beginning of the story. They show where some of her memories may have come from.

Do you remember the story Tomie dePaola told in *The Art Lesson*?

Tracie: Yes. He didn't like doing what he was supposed to do in art class.

Tommy: And he wanted to use his birthday crayons instead of the school crayons.

Mrs. L.: What good memories you have! Do we know if this is a true story?

Rebecca: Yes, because Tomie dePaola did grow up to be an artist.

Ellen: And they show him as a grown-up drawing on the last page.

Mrs. L.: What reason did Tomie dePaola have for writing this story?

Samuel: He wanted to tell us that he has known since he was little that he wanted to be an artist when he grew up. He is an expert at drawing.

Carrie: I think he wanted to tell us that when we know what we really want to do when we grow up, we should practice like he did by drawing pictures everywhere.

Mrs. L.: You have great ideas about Tomie dePaola's art lesson story. Sharing your feelings through a story is another great reason to write a story. Tomie felt proud of his pictures, disappointed by getting only one piece of paper, and excited about going to art class. It's nice to read a story and discover we aren't the only ones in the world who have felt disappointed and to know what makes other people excited and proud of themselves.

Peter Catalanotto's book, *The Painter*, is another story about being an artist. When Peter Catalanotto visited our school, he told us the story about the time his teacher said, "Pete, it looks like you're going to be an artist when you grow up..."

Stevie: But he said, "I'm an artist now," and in the story, his daughter says the same thing. I bet that's why he wrote this story for us to read.

Mrs. L.: Peter Catalanotto told this story because he feels strongly about being an artist. This is another very good reason to write a story. When you feel you have to tell everyone something that has happened to you, it will probably make an excellent story. And it will be an important story to write.

From now on, whenever you feel yourself getting ready to say, "I don't know what to write," think about something that you have done or something that has happened to you. Think about something that makes you feel different or a memory you don't ever want to forget. Then just relax and let the words flow from your mind, down your arm, through your fingertips, out of your pencil, and onto the paper. You are an expert. And once you've written your story down on paper, it will never be forgotten.

Extending the Mini-Lesson

OUR EXPERTS

For our next writers' workshop mini-lesson, I labeled a chart with the words "Experts in Room 4." Below this title, I listed each child's name. When we met for our mini-lesson that day, we listed one experience or topic next to each name. This served to further broaden students' understanding of our unlimited means of expertise.

Experts in Room 4

Matthew	illustrating pictures for book contests
Sean	race cars
Brian	spaghetti
Carrie	birds
Kristen	rotten blond-haired brothers
Brett	mystery stories

ABOUT ME PAGES

Another writers' workshop mini-lesson was spent working on a story idea sheet we call an About Me Page.

I complete an About Me Page on an overhead transparency to stimulate ideas before having students complete a page of their own. (You can copy the blank About Me Page at the end of this chapter.) The page is stapled inside each student's writing folder for easy access during writing time.

Sometimes students draw pictures for their About Me Pages.

Second-Grade About Me Page

First-Grade About Me Page

OTHER GREAT BOOKS

Arthur Writes a Story is an appropriate book to share during a mini-lesson on story ideas. It is also an excellent story for helping young writers acquire a writer's perspective. Marc Brown's Arthur is given a creative writing assignment and learns the importance of telling a story in his own way.

In *Aunt Isabel Tells a Good One*, when Penelope asks her Aunt Isabel to tell her a story, Aunt Isabel obliges. Together, Penelope and Aunt Isabel weave a story with all the magical parts from heroes and villains to a happy ending. This book about writing is two tales in one and a great way to help young writers explore storytelling.

STUDENT PROGRESS

Real-Life Adventures

FIRST-GRADE AUTHOR:

"My Rotten Blond Haired Older Brother" ▶

FIRST-GRADE AUTHOR:

"I Love Spaghetti" ▶

Where Else Do Ideas Come From?

GOAL To explore story inspirations

This mini-lesson helps children identify the endless possibilities of story topics. The morning that I plan to do the lesson, I write the following directions on the board for my students:

Choose a book you like to read.
Think about: Where did the author get this idea for writing?

When we meet for our mini-lesson, I ask students to bring the books they've chosen to our meeting. I begin by reminding my students that there are no right or wrong answers, since the authors of the books are not in the room to tell us the "real" reason for writing a story.

Mrs. L.:   I've asked you to bring a favorite book with you to our writer's meeting, because I want to think about what led these authors to write a particular story. This may help us identify other places to look for story ideas.

Amanda: I picked *The Real Tooth Fairy*. I think the author wrote this book because she wanted other people to know why the tooth fairy looks like everybody's moms and dads.

Ben: Or maybe her mom is the real tooth fairy and that's why she knows the story so well.

Mrs. L.:   Writing a story to tell others something special that you know about is one of the best reasons for writing a story. You work hard because telling the story is important to you.

How about your book, Samuel?

Samuel: I picked *The Toll-Bridge Troll*. At first I thought maybe the author wrote this story because of being bothered by a bully on the way to school. Then I remembered how some stories are a new way of telling an old fairy tale.

Mrs. L.:   Yes, some of our favorite stories are retellings of stories that have been changed or put into a different time and place. *The Toll-Bridge Troll* is a new way of telling...

Class: *The Three Billy Goats Gruff!*

Mrs. L.:   Right! Does anyone else have a story that is a twist on a favorite fairy tale?

Chad: *The True Story of the Three Little Pigs.* I like it, and I think the writer felt sorry for the wolf, so he told the wolf's side of the story.

Mrs. L.:   It certainly gives us another way of looking at the story of *The Three Little Pigs.* Favorite stories are a great place to look for writing ideas. It's fun to take a story you like and change it in some way—maybe put yourself in the story or change the ending. Starting a new story where the other story ended can be fun too. Who has another story idea to share?

Katie: I like *Noisy Nora.* I think the author got mad because nobody was paying any attention to her when she was a little girl. She wrote the story to tell other people about it.

Mrs. L.:   Great thinking! It could be that the author, Rosemary Wells, felt alone or that one of her daughters felt this way. I met Rosemary Wells at a book-signing session one time. She explained how she often uses her daughters' experiences for many of her writing ideas. She may have felt that telling this story was important to let people know they are not alone in feeling a certain way.

Meghan chose one of my favorite stories...

Meghan: I chose *Chrysanthemum.* I think the author was telling readers that it's not nice to make fun of others...

Maddie: ...And that we should be happy being who we are.

Mrs. L.:   I think Kevin Henkes was trying to teach us a lesson with this story. What a great reason to write a story to share with others.

Rebecca: Then maybe if you read the story, you won't be mean like the people who made fun of Chrysanthemum.

Mrs. L.:   Yes. Stories can help us think about the way we treat each other, and stories can help us understand how others feel.

Ryan, you chose *The Bookshop Dog.* Why do you think Cynthia Rylant wrote the story?

Ryan: Because she loves her dog.

Mrs. L.:   I think you're right. Look at the back flap of this book. Here's the author, Cynthia Rylant, and her dog, Martha Jane. Loving something or someone is an excellent reason to write a story.

Ryan: Do you think Martha Jane really went to Hawaii?

Mrs. L.:   I don't know. But I do think Cynthia Rylant knew Martha Jane would make a great idea for a story. Maybe she thought of how difficult it would be to leave Martha Jane and then let her imagination do the rest of the telling.

We've come up with some new places to look for story ideas. When a writer gets an idea for a story, it's called an inspiration. I hope our writers' meeting has given you some inspiration for today's writing time.

Extending the Mini-Lesson

MORE INSPIRATIONS

After doing mini-lessons on "what if's," "Everyone Is an Expert at Something," and "Where Else Do Ideas Come From?," I rarely have students claiming they don't know what to write. They become confident in finding their own topics and eager to explore a new writing possibility.

During our next mini-lesson, I talk more about "inspiration." We discuss how inspiration means having strong feelings about something and how an inspiration often comes to a writer very suddenly, causing him to say, "Now that would make a good story!" We talk about how an inspiration is a writer's feeling that he or she must share a particular idea.

Using the books the students chose for the previous writers' meeting, we compile a list to reflect where story ideas may originate.

Story Inspirations

○ Tell a story ...
- about something special that you know about or that has happened to you.
- to teach a lesson.
- you've heard before in a new way—retell a favorite story.
- to help others understand your feelings.
○
- about something or someone you love.
- to help people think about the way they treat others.

EXPERT AUTHORS' INSPIRATIONS AND DEDICATIONS

On another day, I gather some favorite books that have dedications or notes clearly describing the author's inspiration. This lesson not only highlights additional resources for story inspirations but also gives young writers a taste of the various types of dedications expert authors include in their published books.

For example, in the author's note at the end of *Riptide*, Frances Ward Weller tells of being indebted to a family for their "wonderful, funny, bittersweet tales of their beloved pet."

Jane Yolen dedicated *Owl Moon* to her "husband, who took all of our children owling."

Tomie dePaola dedicated *The Art Lesson* to "my fifth-grade teacher, who always gave me more than one piece of paper..."

Patricia Polacco wrote a story called *My Ol' Man* "in loving memory of William F. Barber, my ol' man."

Gloria Houston wrote *My Great-Aunt Arizona* "for all teachers, members of the most influential profession in the world."

Such examples help illustrate to beginning writers the endless possibilities for story inspirations and often inspire them to write dedications of their own.

A young author's dedication

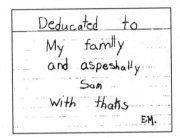

Deducated to
My family
and aspeshally
Sam
with thaks
E.M.

STUDENT HOMEWORK NOTE

After our first week of writers' workshops, I ask my students to copy the following sentence: "My writers' workshop homework is to look for story ideas." In an early parent letter or conference I stress the importance of broadening a child's awareness of writing by:

☼ *showing real-life applications of writing outside the classroom.*

☼ *helping a beginning writer act like a "real author" who is constantly searching for a next writing idea.*

☼ *exploring possible new writing topics.*

Last year, after sending this student homework note to parents, several students came to school with small notebooks for story ideas. One boy, a second grader, carried his notebook everywhere. One day at recess, I found him on the sidelines of the soccer game, writing in his notebook. He raced to show me the page in his notebook that read:

The Day I Scored My First Goal in Soccer

One version of the homework note

AUTHOR VISIT

Whenever possible, I invite a local author in to discuss writing. I ask the author to talk to the students about where ideas come from, how to get started with a new story, and what to do if they are "stuck" with a particular story. I also ask the

author to show a work from rough drafts to finished product. The students are enthused to see someone who gets to write stories for a living and to see the real life applications of writing practice.

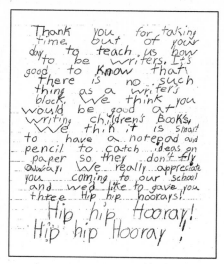

A thank-you note to a visiting author

MEET-THE-AUTHOR VIDEOS

There are excellent videos available through student book clubs that feature interviews with favorite children's authors such as Steven Kellogg and Marc Brown. The videos often show the author in his or her studio. Throughout the interviews, featured authors talk about how they began writing and offer tips for young writers and illustrators. I make these videos a part of our writing mini-lessons, and we focus on that particular author's work during read-aloud times.

IF-YOU-WERE-A-WRITER FOLDERS

Since *If You Were a Writer* is a great inspiration for our writers' workshop, I highlighted the key points of the book for future reference (see page 42). I copy a sheet for each student to decorate and then glue the sheet to the front of each writing folder. Every so often, we reread the inspirations from *If You Were a Writer* that helped us to begin seeing ourselves as writers.

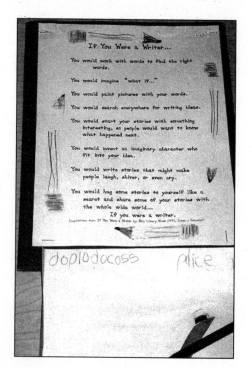

A student writing folder

Sharing Stories

GOAL To share stories with an audience

*T*he writing process must involve sharing, since all writers grow as a result of hearing what others think about their writing efforts. Having an audience helps beginning writers match their writing to their purposes for writing. For example, if a student wants a story to evoke laughter, and the audience doesn't laugh, the student quickly sees the need for editing.

For many children, getting up and speaking in front of an audience can be an intimidating and uncomfortable experience—especially when they're sharing the kinds of personal stories they frequently write in a writers' workshop. So sharing stories in a whole-group situation is optional in my classroom. I don't force the issue of sharing until children volunteer. And I've found that even those students who are the most apprehensive eventually write something they're excited about sharing. Many times, students gain the confidence to share their work by seeing classmates succeed at it.

Reading a story to the whole class is only one way of sharing. Some students are more comfortable reading their work with a partner in a Sharing Corner or with me during a writing conference. Others prefer displaying work in the hallway.

Without modeling and guidance, students tend to think sharing a story means reading it, having the audience clap, and sitting down again. However, sharing to become a better writer involves getting feedback from your audience about ways to improve a piece of written work. Young children have to learn how to give and receive appropriate criticism, and establishing a comfortable environment for giving suggestions and comments is crucial. As I mentioned in Chapter One, I begin the year by sharing a story of my own to model what sharing looks like and to prove that our classroom community is a safe place to share.

The lesson in which I demonstrate my first piece of writing to the class and prove the value of sharing a story usually looks something like this:

Mrs. L.: Today for our writers' meeting, I'd like to share my story with you. It's about reading a book on a rainy day. I'm certain you will be a respectful and polite audience since I need your help to make my story even better. Tell me what a respectful and polite audience looks like.

Carrie: We sit quietly while you read your story.

Mrs. L.: Yes, to be a good listener, it helps to sit quietly. I'll know you were a good listener if you can tell me details about my story when I'm finished. What else?

Brett: We should clap when you finish reading your story if we like it.

Mrs. L.:	I hope you do like my story. What if you don't enjoy my story?
Colleen:	We should still clap. It's nice, and it might hurt your feelings if we don't.
Mrs. L.:	I guarantee my feelings *would* be hurt if you didn't clap. What would a polite audience do if I make a mistake in my writing or my reading?
Meghan:	We smile and let you fix your mistake. It would hurt your feelings if we laughed.
Mrs. L.:	Oh, thank you. I feel less nervous knowing you won't laugh at my mistakes. Please laugh if my story is funny, but don't laugh if I make a mistake.
	Remember, you'll all have a chance to share your stories with an audience. If you respect the feelings of other writers, they will be respectful of you.
	My story is called "Rainy Days." Please listen carefully for sentences you like and sentences you would change if you were the writer.
	(I read my story to the class, purposely making mistakes along the way.)
Mrs. L.:	What did you think of my story?
Stevie:	I liked it.
Mrs. L.:	Thank you. What did you like?
Stevie:	I liked the whole thing.
Mrs. L.:	I'm glad you liked my story, but as a writer I need to know what kinds of sentences or words you liked in my story so that I'll be sure to write those kinds of sentences again. Was there a particular sentence that you liked?
Stevie:	I liked the part where your cat fell off the window ledge onto the pillow, because that made me laugh.
Mrs. L.:	Thank you for remembering that detail. I'll try to add more sentences to make you laugh. Anything else?
Meghan:	I liked when you wrote about the "muddy chocolate lab footprints."
Mrs. L.:	Great. What did you like about that sentence?
Meghan:	It was like those sentences Melia tried to think of in *If You Were a Writer*.
Mrs. L.:	Melia called those "words that paint pictures." I'll try to write more sentences that paint pictures.
	Was there any part of my story that you didn't understand or an improvement you think I should make?
Tommy:	I like it just the way it is.
Mrs. L.:	Thank you. You know, as a writer it wouldn't hurt my feelings if you told me about something you didn't understand in my story or about a part you didn't like. I want you to tell me about parts I need to improve. If you consider my feelings and make a suggestion in a friendly way, I can become a better writer.
Stevie:	O.K., I may have thought of a different title.
Mrs. L.:	Great! What's your suggestion.
Stevie:	What about "The Rainy Day Dog?"

Mrs. L.:	I like that. Thank you for that suggestion.
Lauren:	What about "The Muddy Day Dog?"
Mrs. L.:	Another good idea! These are very helpful suggestions. I 'll think more about a new title.

As a writer, it's nice to know what my audience likes. I like the challenge of making my story even better. So now that I've shared my story with you, I'll also try to add more sentences with words that paint pictures like Meghan suggested or funny sentences like Stevie suggested. Now I have more writing to do. Rewriting to make the story even better is an important part of sharing.

Thank you for being a polite audience. You waited patiently without laughing when I made a mistake. You listened carefully to remember details from sentences you liked and suggestions for improving my story. I know we will all become better writers if we continue to have such a helpful audience.

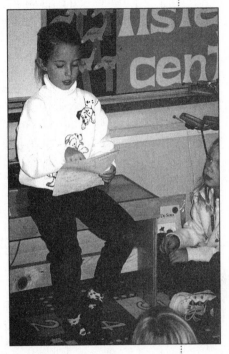

A writer shares a story.

Extending the Mini-Lesson

MORE SHARING

With practice, my students get better at verbalizing suggestions to fellow writers. I continue to model how to phrase constructive criticism, and I share improvements I make to my stories based upon their advice.

To reinforce good sharing techniques, we share stories as a whole class during one mini-lesson each week until I feel confident the students have good sharing habits. This whole-group sharing is valuable for addressing certain issues together. When an issue arises in a small-group sharing session, I make a note of it and share it during a future mini-lesson. Students quickly learn that comments such as "I liked the whole story" are not readily accepted when I consistently ask them to clarify what they especially liked about a story.

I am an active participant in the sharing groups, spending time with each group and giving examples of parts of each story I enjoy and the reasons I like them. Soon, the students are able to verbalize their favorite kinds of sentences and coach each other during sharing time.

ROLE PLAY: MORE MODELS

During another mini-lesson, a student volunteer helps me role-play how to share a story in a Sharing Corner during writing time. The student begins the demonstration by tapping me on the shoulder while I pretend to be busy writing. The partner whispers, "Would you like to listen to my story?" Together, we choose a Sharing Corner. The partner quietly reads her story to me. I model giving a specific compliment, a suggestion for improvement, and another compliment.

If time allows, I choose students to model the inappropriate way to use a Sharing Corner by using a loud voices, talking about recess, and being inattentive to the reader. This example makes a lasting impression and opens up a discussion of ways to deal with an inattentive audience.

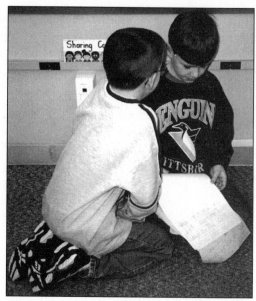

Students share a story in a Sharing Corner.

To help students use sharing time fairly, I place a checklist beside each sharing circle location with the names of the students in that sharing group. After a student shares a story, he places a check next to his name. This student then chooses the next person to share by looking at the list for a person with the fewest check marks. This checklist system prevents disagreements about who's next, makes me aware of who has and has not shared, and helps parent volunteers offer fair sharing time.

The Writing Conference

CONFIDENCE-BUILDING

When I meet individually with a child, we sit at a table with erasers, pencils, and the box of favorite books. While parent helpers are assisting the other writers with sound-spelling and story concerns during writing time, I hold individual student writing conferences. I usually manage to meet with two to four students a day. When I meet with students during the initial writers' workshop conference, my key role is that of confidence builder. I'm establishing a comfortable environment for sharing, building trust, and showing my genuine interest in each student's writing efforts. We talk about where the idea for each story originated. As a student reads a story with me, I listen without jotting down comments, giving each writer my full attention.

When a student has difficulty reading a part of the story because of phonetic

spelling, I simply say, "Tell me what happened next," encouraging the writer to interpret the story orally. I remind students that writing and reading their own stories will become easier with practice and that it's okay to add words that they forgot or wish they'd written. Often this initial conference entails phonetically spelling a difficult word together. We make sure all the main sounds of a difficult word are included in a student's "invented" spelling. I remind capable students to check for the "book-spelling" of a word that may have been part of a weekly spelling list.

I like to I impress upon my beginning writers that "if you can say it, you can write it." I never want a writer to give up writing a wonderful idea because of an intimidating word—particularly those early writers whose oral language exceeds their fine-motor skills.

I show each student that I am genuinely interested in him or her as a writer by giving illustrative, specific compliments, such as "you sound-spelled this word using all the main sounds" to an early beginning writer or "the words in this sentence paint a picture" to a more advanced writer. Meaningful praise is specific and provides an example to substantiate the compliment and verify the writer's accomplishment. Even first and second graders are quick to pick up on the insincerity of a general comment such as "What a good writer you are!"

EXAMPLES OF MEANINGFUL PRAISE

- ☼ You spelled this word using all the main sounds.
- ☼ This sentence paints a picture.
- ☼ You spelled this word with book-spelling.
- ☼ Your illustration goes well with your words. I especially like...
- ☼ This sentence reminds me of something that happened to me...
- ☼ You put the right amount of space between your words in this sentence.
- ☼ Your beginning sentence makes me want to read more to find out...
- ☼ I like the way you had the characters talking to one another.

We take each accomplishment a step further by improving another sentence in the same way—"Let's try to get all the sounds in the word *alligator*" or "Let's paint a picture of your little brother in this sentence"—to extend a good writing technique.

We end our initial writing conference by referring to the child's About Me Page and discussing possibilities for the next writing idea. As the student goes back to his seat, I write the date of his initial conference on my class chart for writers' workshop, along with a few words about our meeting.

Tracie's Conference, Grade 2

Mrs. L.:	What story would you like to share with me today?
Tracie:	"The Continuing of Stellaluna Writes a Story."
Mrs. L.:	What an interesting title. What inspired you to write this story?
Tracie:	Two books: *Stellaluna* and *Arthur Writes a Story*.
Mrs. L.:	Those are great books. Please read your story to me.

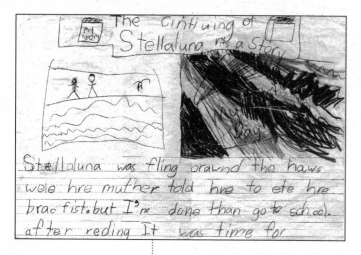

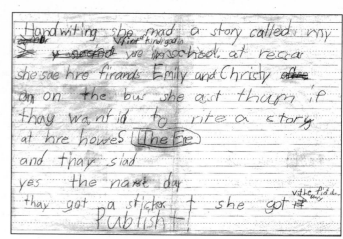

"The Continuing of Stellaluna Writes a Story"

Mrs. L.: I enjoyed your story, Tracie. I especially like the way you had Stellaluna flying around the house and her mom telling her she had to eat her breakfast before school. I like how you said Stellaluna and her friends got the story published. What a happy ending. Since your story was about Stellaluna's story, I was wondering what she wrote about.

Tracie: It was about her first year of kindergarten.

Mrs. L.: You wrote, "She made a story." Let's add the words "called 'My First Day of Kindergarten.'"

Tracie: O.K. I think I can spell "kindergarten."

Mrs. L.: Your sharing group would enjoy hearing this story. Would you like to share "Stellaluna Writes a Story" during sharing time?

Tracie: Yes, but first I want to fix the sentence about her story.

Mrs. L.: Good idea. We'll fix it together. I know we can tackle "kindergarten."

(After changing the sentence, we continue.)

Let's take a look at your About Me Page. Do you have an idea for your next story?

Tracie: I'm not sure...I like the idea about the land of magic. I saw a show on TV, and I was going to change the idea.

Mrs. L.: I think the land of magic would be a great idea for your next story. Thank you for sharing your story with me.

Writers' Workshop

Tracie 10/2 Developing Ideas	Colleen 10/2 Help with Sound spelling
Sean 10/3 Simple Sentences	Mark 10/3 Spacing between words
Amanda	Carrie
Sara - 10/3 Puts extra sounds in words	Ryan
Brett	Lauren 10/5 Uses complex ideas

Initial Conference Recording Blocks

Name _____

About Me Page

Things I like to do:

1. _____

2. _____

3. _____

4. _____

Places I like to go:

1. _____

2. _____

3. _____

4. _____

Things from my imagination:

1. _____

2. _____

3. _____

4. _____

Fun times I've had with family and friends:

1. _____

2. _____

3. _____

4. _____

If You Were a Writer...

⭐ You would work with words to find the right words.

⭐ You would imagine "what if..."

⭐ You would paint pictures with your words.

⭐ You would search everywhere for writing ideas.

⭐ You would start your stories with something interesting, so people would want to know what happened next.

⭐ You would invent an imaginary character who fit into your idea.

⭐ You would write stories that might make people laugh, shiver, or even cry.

⭐ You would hug some stories to yourself like a secret and share some stories with the whole wide world...

if you were a writer.

 Inspirations from *If You Were a Writer* by Joan Lowery Nixon (Simon & Schuster, 1995)   *Literature-Based Mini-Lessons to Teach Writing*   Scholastic Professional Books

Books to Use: Getting the Workshop Started

Brandenberg, A. (1996). *Those Summers.* New York: HarperCollins Publishers.

Brown, M. (1996). *Arthur Writes a Story.* New York: Little, Brown and Company.

Cannon, J. (1993). *Stellaluna.* New York: Harcourt Brace & Company.

Catalanotto, P. (1995). *The Painter.* New York: Orchard Books.

dePaola, T. (1989). *The Art Lesson.* New York: G. P. Putnam's Sons.

Duke, K. (1992). *Aunt Isabel Tells a Good One.* New York: Puffin Unicorn Books.

Henkes, K. (1991). *Chrysanthemum.* New York: Greenwillow Books.

Houston, G. (1992). *My Great-Aunt Arizona.* New York: HarperCollins Publishers.

Kaye, M. (1990). *The Real Tooth Fairy.* New York: Harcourt Brace & Company.

Kovacs, D., Preller, J. (1991). *Meet the Authors and Illustrators: Volume One.* New York: Scholastic Inc.

———— (1993). *Meet the Authors and Illustrators: Volume Two.* New York: Scholastic Inc.

Nixon, J. (1995). *If You Were a Writer.* New York: Simon & Schuster.

Polacco, P. (1995). *My Ol' Man.* New York: Philomel Books.

———— (1994). *My Rotten Redheaded Older Brother.* New York: Simon & Schuster.

Rylant, C. (1996). *The Bookshop Dog.* New York: Blue Sky Press.

Scieszka, J. (1989). *The True Story of the Three Little Pigs.* New York: Penguin Books.

Weller, F. (1990). *Riptide.* New York: Putnam & Grosset Group.

Wells, R. (1973). *Noisy Nora.* New York: Dial Books.

Wolff, P. (1995). *The Toll-Bridge Troll.* New York: Harcourt Brace & Company.

Yolen, J. (1987). *Owl Moon.* New York: Philomel Books.

Exploring Story Leads

CHAPTER 3

The Mini-Lessons

The Story Begins...

Improving the Lead

The Setting: Time and Place

The Writing Goals

To explore beginning sentences

To improve story leads

To explore story settings

Favorite Books to Use

Books with interesting first sentences, such as:
The Crack of Dawn Walkers by Amy Hest
Feathers for Lunch by Lois Ehlert
The Frog Prince Continued by Jon Scieszka
Harry, the Dirty Dog by Gene Zion
Owl Moon by Jane Yolen
The Purple Coat by Amy Hest

The Favorite Books Box

Books with distinct settings, such as:
Arthur's Teacher Trouble by Marc Brown
Babushka Baba Yaga by Patricia Polacco
Funny, Funny Lyle by Bernard Waber
Goldilocks and the Three Bears by Jan Brett
Swamp Angel by Anne Isaacs

The Story Begins...

GOAL To explore beginning sentences

Early in the school year as I was glancing through the children's writing folders, I noticed that nearly half of the students' stories began with "Hello, my name is..." and the other half began with "This is a ..." I realized then that I needed to help my first and second graders explore story leads and discover the importance of exciting beginning sentences.

Since I'd been writing a story during writers' workshop about walking my dog, I reached for the book The Crack of Dawn Walkers. *To establish a comfortable environment for sharing and improving writing, I jotted down in my easel-sized notebook my own simple story beginning and a more descriptive lead for comparison, ready for our next mini-lesson in writing.*

Mrs. L.:   You know I've been writing a story about walking my dog, Sydney, because that's one of my favorite things to do in the fall. But I am not fond of my beginning. I thought of the book *The Crack of Dawn Walkers* by Amy Hest, since her story is also about getting up early and walking.

Rebecca: But her book doesn't have a dog in it.

Mrs. L.:   You're right, but I like the words she uses and thought she might give me some good ideas for my own writing.

Katie: I like the way Sadie orders hot cocoa with double whipped cream in that book.

Mrs. L.:   Well, let's see if Amy Hest can help with my story beginning. Her story begins:

> ***Grandfather taps on her bedroom door. "Are you up?" he calls softly. "It's time!" Sadie kicks at the worn pink blanket, and the toasty sheet with stripes. Her feet skim the cold wood floor as she races for the rocker, and the woolen knee socks she left hanging the night before.***

I like the way Amy Hest makes you feel like you're in the room with Sadie, seeing what she's doing. After reading her beginning, I changed my story from:

This is my dog, Sydney. Every Saturday we go for a walk.

to:

At 6:00, Sydney stood beside my bed with her leash dangling from her mouth. Her skinny brown tail was wagging back and forth like a windshield wiper. "It's Saturday, Syd! Couldn't you wait until 7:00?" I ask her, rolling over, trying to ignore the whimpering chocolate lab at my bedside.

Sara: My dog drags her leash in her mouth when we walk too.

Mrs. L.: Then my story beginning makes you think of something that has happened to you before.

Ben: Yes, and I can see her tail wagging like a windshield wiper.

Lauren: I like how you talk to Sydney in the beginning. In your first beginning, you didn't talk.

Mrs. L.: I thought talking might make it more exciting. Does my story make you want to read more?

Ben: Yes, I wonder if you get out of bed and take her for a walk or go back to sleep.

Lauren: It's a story about walking, so I hope you get up and take Sydney for a walk!

Mrs. L.: Good idea! It's a challenge to make your beginning sentences more exciting. Let's take a look at how some authors started a few of our favorite stories. Let's see how they grabbed our attention to make us want to read more. I'll read a first sentence while you close your eyes. Try to guess the book with each beginning sentence. Here's the first one…

"Uh-oh."

Tracie: I'm not sure.

Mrs. L.: Does this beginning make you want to read more?

Class: Yes!

Tommy: I want to know why the author wrote "Uh- Oh."

Dana: That means there's a problem.

Mrs. L.: I agree. Here's the next sentence: "Door's left open, just a crack."

Stevie: *Birds for Lunch!*

Mrs. L.: Close…*Feathers for Lunch.* Is this a good first sentence?

Meghan: Yes, because I know the cat gets out and since it's called *Feathers for Lunch,* the first time I heard the book I wondered if the cat would eat a bird for lunch.

Mrs. L.: I did, too. Here's another first sentence that grabbed my attention when I read it. Close your eyes. "Well, let's just say they lived sort of happily for a long time."

Matthew: It's good because you want to read to find out why they're sort of happy.

Mrs. L.: It's not "once upon a time" like most fairy tales begin. It's different, so it grabs our attention.

Amanda: That's from *The Frog Prince Continued*.

Mrs. L.: You're right! Jon Scieszka probably didn't write "Well, let's just say they lived sort of happily for a long time" on his first try. I bet he changed it—maybe several times—to make it more exciting. When we meet in our sharing circles today, let's share our story beginnings and how we changed them to make our audience want to read more.

Extending the Mini-Lesson

ONGOING CHARTS...

At read-aloud time that afternoon, we created a chart where we recorded the first sentences of some of our favorite books. As the year progressed, our ongoing list grew longer and longer, reflecting the many styles of story beginnings.

Story Beginnings

- It was late one winter night, long past my bedtime, when Pa and I went owling. (*Owl Moon*, Yolen)

- Harry was a white dog with black spots who liked everything, except...getting a bath. (*Harry the Dirty Dog*, Zion)

- Prowlpuss is cunning and wily and sly, a king-size cat with one ear and one eye. (*Prowlpuss*, Wilson)

- "Is your mama a llama?" I asked my friend Dave. (*Is Your Mama a Llama?*, Guarino)

- Leo couldn't do anything right. (*Leo the Late Bloomer*, Kraus)

- Sylvester Duncan lived with his mother and father on Acorn Road in Oatsdale. (*Sylvester and the Magic Pebble*, Steig)

- Arthur's sister D.W. had a problem. (*Arthur Babysits*, Brown)

- When I was young in the mountains, Grandfather came home in the evening covered with the black dust of a coal mine. (*When I Was Young in the Mountains*, Rylant,)

- Louise Jenkins and I love horses, but we aren't allowed to have real ones. (*Best Friends*, Kellogg)

Each time we added a sentence to our list, we briefly discussed how the words grabbed our attention by giving details of where the story begins, telling us the character's feelings—all making us want to know more.

Shortly after our initial lesson on story beginnings, I began a mini-lesson with the children gathered around a second chart labeled "More Excellent Beginnings." We discussed the cleverness of these beginnings and soon discovered the authors were members of our own writers' workshop:

More Excellent Beginnings

- Once upon a moonlit night there was a warm and shadowy cave. (Meghan)

- On a breezy, misty summer night, I heard a rumbling sound outside my window. (Tommy)

- On a breezy fall morning, I slowly woke up. (Amanda)

- The big day was coming, and Deann just couldn't wait. (Kristen)

- It was a dark, dark night when the cupcakes began to fly. (Brian)

These two charts of story beginnings, hanging side by side on our classroom wall, support the use of children's literature as the basis of mini-lessons in writing. The children and their teacher, impressed by their accomplishments, smile proudly, knowing the authors of children's literature will lend them an idea or two when it comes to beginning stories of their own.

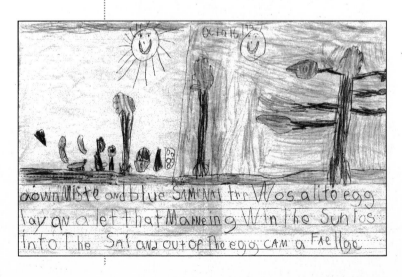

◀ FIRST-GRADE AUTHOR

INSPIRATION: *THE VERY HUNGRY CATERPILLAR*

One misty and blue summer night there was a little egg laying on a leaf...

MECHANICS: SPACING BETWEEN WORDS

For beginning writers, who require so much concentration and effort to write the simplest of ideas, the mechanics are less important than the ideas. But when students are ready to handle both the ideas and certain mechanics, such as proper spacing between words, examples from our Favorite Books Box make the lessons more fun.

Many of my first-grade writers begin the year running all of their words together.

The following lesson helps students see the importance of using proper spacing when they write. I copy the first page of *Goldilocks and the Three Bears* on the board as follows:

Onceuponatimetherewerethreebearswholivedtogetherinahouse

oftheirowninawoodOneofthemwasalittle,small,weebear,and

onewasamiddlesizedbear,andtheotherwasagreat,hugebear.

Mrs. L.:	Today I wanted to share the first page from one of my favorite books. It's *Goldilocks and the Three Bears* by Jan Brett. I copied the first page on the overhead for you to see. Here it is.
Ben:	That doesn't look right.
Rebecca:	You forgot the spaces.
Mrs. L.:	Oh, dear. Is this a problem?
Amanda:	No, we can probably figure it out.
Dana:	It would be easier with the spaces. We'll just have to sound out where the words should be. Usually this story begins with "Once upon a time."
Mrs. L.:	Good idea. I'll draw lines between the words if you tell me where the spaces should be placed.

Meghan: Upon begins with *u*, so *once* ends with *e*.

Mrs. L.: I'll draw a line between *e* and *u*. *Upon* ends with the *n* sound, so I think I know where the next line belongs.

Matthew: Between the *n* and the *a*. Put another line after the *a* because that's the next word.

Mrs. L.: Like this?

Class: Yes.

Mrs. L.: What's next? Once upon a...

Class: Time.

Tommy: *Time* ends with the *m* sound.

Mrs. L.: Right, but it has a silent *e* at the end so I'll put the line after the *e*, not the *m*...

We continue in this manner with the rest of the sentence. I end the lesson by demonstrating how to write a few words on lined paper using a "two-finger space" between each word.

"two-finger spacing" between words

Improving the Lead

GOAL To improve story leads

During individual conferences with the children, I identify a few students who are still writing basic beginning sentences. Since the children are developing an awareness of the kinds of sentences that grab their attention, I explain that they need to focus on the first few sentences so that their wonderful story ideas will be more detailed, and the audience won't lose interest. With the writers' permission, I copy one sentence at the top of separate overhead transparencies and, one at a time, we share each beginning. The children's fellow writers are eager to help them improve their story leads. What follows is the heart of the mini-lesson in which beginning writers work cooperatively to improve a story lead.

One day I was flying my kite. Then a big gust of wind came along and took my kite right out of the grasp of my hands and into the air. I ran back...

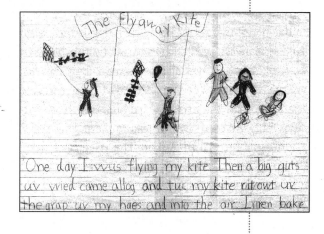

Mrs. L.:	Today we are going to look at story leads. The lead is the first few sentences of a story—the sentences that lead the reader into the story, that make the reader feel a part of the story. Let's look at Rebecca's lead.
Rebecca:	My story is about my birthday party, so I wrote "My birthday is in January."
Mrs. L.:	You must be excited, and that makes your birthday an excellent idea for writing. Can you think of any stories we've heard about birthdays?
Ellen:	*Arthur's Birthday!*
Mrs. L.:	Good thinking! How does that story begin? Stevie, would you get *Arthur's Birthday* from the Favorite Books Box and read the beginning that Marc Brown wrote?

Stevie:	"I can't wait! I can't wait!"
Mrs. L.:	What do you think of this beginning?
Sara:	I think that Arthur is excited. I wonder what Arthur can't wait for. I bet it's his birthday.
Mrs. L.:	Does this give you any ideas to help Rebecca with her beginning?
Matthew:	She could say, "I can't wait. I can't wait."
Dana:	But that's copying Marc Brown. Maybe she counted the days on the calendar.
Mrs. L.:	That's a nice idea. What do you think Rebecca?
Rebecca:	I could write: "I counted the days on the calendar. Yeah! My birthday is in three more days! I can't wait."
Mrs. L.:	That really adds details to your beginning.
Ellen:	Maybe she could add to the very beginning. "1, 2, 3, I counted the days..." That would show she was really counting.
Mrs. L.:	What do you think Rebecca?
Rebecca:	I like that beginning even better.
Mrs. L.:	Ryan is writing about his birthday, too. He began: "My birthday is in October."
Lauren:	Well, since October is in the fall he could start it with the leaves changing.
Katie:	Like *The Purple Coat*.
Mrs. L.:	Let's see how Amy Hest got her story started...

Every fall, when the leaves start melting into pretty purples and reds and those bright golden shades of pumpkin, Mama says, "Coat Time, Gabrielle!"

Meghan:	How about if Ryan writes, "Every October when the leaves start changing into pretty colors..."
Stevie:	"...and falling to the ground." That would make it good.
Ryan:	Well, maybe I "jump in a pile of leaves."
Tommy:	And say it's your birthday!
Ryan:	Okay. Thanks!
Stephanie:	But I bet he screams it's his birthday.
Mrs. L.:	Good word. What do you think, Ryan?
Ryan:	I think I'll use *yells*.
Amanda:	Colleen and I are writing a story together. We were going to write: "the sun was shining in the window" but then I thought of the words beating down. The sun does that.
Mrs. L.:	Those extra words make the sentence easy to imagine. It is a good idea to put yourself in the beginning of your story, to imagine what is happening all around you. Challenge yourself to write just a few more words to give extra details and make the story lead extra special. Maybe there is a favorite book that can help you write your beginning...

By the end of writers' workshop that day, Rebecca's lead had evolved into:

1, 2, 3. I counted the days on the calendar. "I can't wait! I can't wait!" "Why?" asked my little sister, Lilly. "Because my birthday is just three days away."

The other students were anxious to hear her additions and encouraged her to keep writing. Rebecca, who often lost interest in her writing efforts, was motivated by her friends' involvement, so she put more time and effort into writing the story "I Can't Wait."

Ryan's birthday story lead became:

One day in October when the leaves change colors and fall to the ground, Ryan jumps in a pile of leaves. "It's my birthday!" I yell.

We continued with this pattern of sharing a beginning, identifying a similar tradebook and together adding details to make the lead more exciting or different. The children's story leads proved to me that borrowing ideas and images from the "experts" is effective.

"Like all writers, children incorporate in their compositions bits and pieces of what they have heard and read in the works of others."

The Beginnings of Writing by Temple, Nathan, Temple, & Burris;
Allyn and Bacon, 1993

Extending the Mini-Lesson

OTHER EXAMPLES...

One day shortly after hearing *The Purple Coat*, Katie said, "I'm going to write a story about getting a new coat too." She wrote this beginning to her story called "The Jelly-Bean-Black, Grassy-Green, Apple-Red and Sky-Blue Coat":

Whenever the earth got cold and it was winter, a little girl named Courtney had to get a new coat.

Lauren began her version of "The Tangerine Coat" on the same day:

On autumn days on Oakdale Avenue, when the leaves turn that pretty shade of red and orange and when the acorns fall, mama says "time to get a new red coat."

For several weeks, our mini-lessons involved sharing the first attempts at story beginnings and the ways students could change them to make them more exciting. During sharing time from now on, we evaluate the effectiveness of each story lead.

Gradually, the students became more confident about creating good beginning sentences, often erasing the first sentence several times or using a caret to add more words. Now most were excited by the challenge of story leads. They'd raise their hands more frequently, saying "I want to read my beginning sentences to you" or "I've got a great lead." I continued to be amazed at what these young writers were capable of creating, and I knew that our "experts" were playing a major role in building their confidence and in giving them a new reason to listen to the daily read-aloud stories.

PEACEFUL IN THE FOREST UNTIL

One day I was walking in the woods and was whistling a little tune. It was real sunny. There were big oak trees and pine. It was a wonderful picture until...

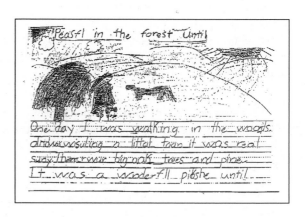

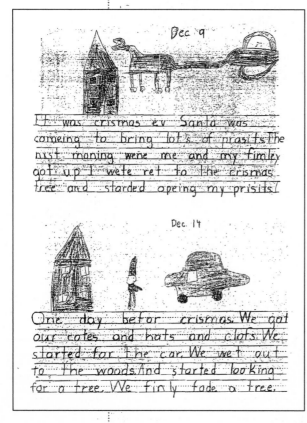

CHRISTMAS STORY LEADS:

Dec. 9: It was Christmas Eve. Santa was coming to bring lots of presents...

Dec. 14: One day before Christmas, we got our coats, and hats and gloves. We started for the car.

The Setting: Time and Place

GOAL To explore story settings

O ne afternoon in December, we were making a story map of Goldilocks and the Three Bears, and I discovered that the children could readily identify the setting of the story. So I decided to extend this concept to a writers' workshop mini-lesson. This activity evolved into one of my favorite lessons for beginning writers. I select a variety of books with rather obvious settings and place our math floor graph and some index cards on the carpet.

Mrs. L.: We've talked about how putting yourself in the place of your story helps make your story more detailed and often easier to write. I'd like you to help me identify where these stories take place. Then we will organize them on our floor graph. Who remembers what the place of the story is called?

David: The setting?

Mrs. L.: Good! Where the story takes place is part of the setting. What else makes up the setting?

Sara: If the story takes place long ago or takes place today.

Mrs. L.: Yes, we call that time. So, setting is *time* and *place*, or, *when* and *where*. Let's look at these books and decide which time and place these authors used when they wrote each story.

Here's a favorite, *Swamp Angel*. When does this story take place?

Carrie: Long ago. In pioneer days.

Mrs. L.: Good! Where does the story take place?

Ellen: In the country.

Mrs. L.: Excellent. Let's put *Swamp Angel* on the first row of our floor graph and label it "Long Ago in the Country." What about the story *Babushka Baba Yaga*?

Class: Long ago.

Samuel: Long ago and outside.

Mrs. L.: Long ago is right. Does it take place outside in the city?

Class: No, the country.

Mrs. L.:	Okay, we'll place *Babushka Baba Yaga* with "Long Ago in the Country" too.
Brett:	I think *Goldilocks and the Three Bears* goes in that row.
Mrs. L.:	That's a great idea. What about *Funny, Funny Lyle*? The story begins on East 88th Street.
Dana:	That's a city, because cities have lots of streets. I know because my aunt lives in Philadelphia. Lyle, the crocodile, must live in the city.
Mrs. L.:	You're right. Lyle lives in the city, not in the country like Baba Yaga or Goldilocks. Does the cover of this book look like long ago?
Brett:	No, those kids are dressed like us. That looks like today.
Mrs. L.:	I agree. There's a *p* word that means the same as today. Does anyone know the word?
Tommy:	Now means today. But it's not a *p* word.
Mrs. L.:	Right. Here's another hint. You also get this *p* word wrapped up on your birthday...
Tommy:	A present?
Kristen:	Oh! The present time means "today."
Mrs. L.:	Great! So the new row of our graph should say...
Ben:	In the present day, in the city.
Mrs. L.:	You got it! Can you find another "Present Day in the City" story?
Kristen:	*Nana's Birthday Party.* I think Nana lives in the city.
Dana:	No, that's the country.
Mrs. L.:	Let's look and see. It could be country, but look at this picture where Brette is painting. Look outside the window...
Dana:	Oh, those are skyscrapers. It's a city setting.
Mrs. L.:	I think *Nana's Birthday Party* is another "Present Day in the City" story. Let's try a story we read not too long ago—*Arthur's Teacher Trouble*. What is the setting of this favorite book?
Ben:	That looks like today, so it's the present day.
Stevie:	Part of it's in school and part of it is outside. Remember when he's in his tree house?
Mrs. L.:	Yes, and here's a page from inside Arthur's house.
Meghan:	It doesn't look like a city. Maybe in the country.
Colleen:	Maybe we should call it a neighborhood, because neighborhoods have schools and houses.
Mrs. L.:	Present day in a neighborhood?
Class:	Yes!
Mrs. L.:	Do you see any other stories on the chalk ledge that have present day, neighborhood settings?
Lauren:	The *Crack of Dawn Walkers* could take place in a neighborhood.
Mrs. L.:	The cover shows Grandpa and Sadie walking in a snowy place.
Carrie:	That looks like a neighborhood, since there aren't tall buildings like the city.

Mrs. L.:   I agree. I'll put *The Crack of Dawn Walkers* with *Arthur's Teacher Trouble*. What do you think about this favorite book, *My Great-Aunt Arizona?*

Meghan: I love that book. I think it takes place in the country.

Mrs. L.:   Long ago or present day?

Class: Long ago.

Mrs. L.:   Great! What about *Two Cool Cows?*

Ellen: That is on a farm.

Rebecca: So, it's not in the city. Maybe a neighborhood.

Sara: My Grandma lives on a farm and it's not really in a neighborhood. It's all by itself.

Mrs. L.:   So if the setting is not the city, and we're not sure if we should call it a neighborhood...

Samuel: I bet it's in the country.

Mrs. L.:   Good thinking. Present day or long ago?

Samuel: I think it's present day. The kids' clothes look like today.

Rebecca: It's not too long ago like *Goldilocks*.

Meghan: But it might be the same time as *My Great-Aunt Arizona* except that the cows are wearing sunglasses.

Mrs. L.:   Let's put *Two Cool Cows* with "Present Day in the Country." Do you see any other stories with a setting where the place is the country rather than a neighborhood?

Ben: The cover of *High-Wire Henry* looks like it's in the mountains.

Mrs. L.:   Let's look inside for a neighborhood.

Ben: It looks like that house is by itself in the country.

Mrs. L.:   Okay, I'll place *High-Wire Henry* with "Present Day in the Country" too. Any other long ago stories?

Amanda: *Bub* is in a castle so it's probably long ago in the country.

Dana: Yes, there weren't cities long ago.

Mrs. L.:   Great. Any others?

Stevie: *Yankee Doodle* is long ago in the country too.

Mrs. L.:   You're very good at naming the settings of stories. Think about the stories you are writing. Does your story fit into one of these groups of settings? If you haven't put your character in a certain place or if you can't picture the setting of your story, go back to the beginning and add a sentence or two to tell *where* and *when* your story takes place. We'll try to name the settings during sharing time today.

   But first, let's try to name the settings of a few more favorite books.

   How about *Berlioz the Bear* and *Dogzilla?*

Extending the Mini-Lesson

EXPANDING THE GRAPH

We continue organizing our favorite books by setting, often beginning future mini-lessons by naming the setting of the book we read for read-aloud the previous day. With my guidance, we label each row using the children's language. Our goal is to search for books to complete the rows of our graph. I eventually transfer these books from the floor graph to a chart that can be hung on the wall. We continue to classify the stories we read according to their setting, adding new descriptors as needed.

The graph we completed for story settings

During story sharing time, I ask the writer to identify the setting of a particular story. This question often requires that the writer return to a story lead and provide the audience with more information. The student's knowledge of and vocabulary for discussing and appreciating literature expands with hints from fellow beginning writers and the expert writers we invited into our classroom. The authors of children's literature continued to help us grow as writers.

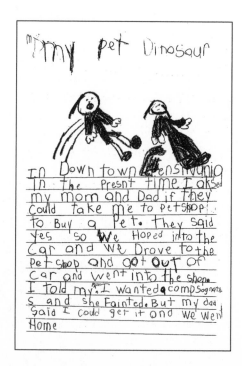

This first-grade author's story has a clear setting of time and place.

The Writing Conference

STORY LEADS

At a story-lead conference, as the student reads a story, I write the beginning sentence in my notebook of anecdotal records. I reserve one page for each child's beginning sentences and the child's rating of these sentences on a scale from one to ten. If their self-rating is low, we find a book to help us improve the sentence. We refer to these sentences frequently, and as the year progresses, the children are often surprised at their progress when they compare their favorite sentences. During story sharing times, beginning sentences are a focal point for listening and discussing.

MANAGEMENT TIP

Keep copies of the Beginning Sentences form at the end of this chapter on a clipboard to record beginning sentences as you're walking around the room or listening to stories students are sharing. At a glance, you and the writer will be able to see how his beginning sentences are improving with practice.

Sara 's Beginning Sentences   Date **Oct. 19**
                                                Self-Rating: **3/7**

1st Try: **One day when I woke up I heard a noise.**

2nd Try: **One breezy fall day when I woke up I hurried out of bed and I heard a noise.**

Since the story lead is more than just the first attention-grabbing sentence, I ask the writer to tell me more. I may ask: "Was it a sunny or stormy day?" "Were you walking quickly or dragging your feet?" "Were you happy or sad?" Such questions help children add sentences that support their beginning sentences. To cut down on erasing, I take this opportunity to demonstrate the use of the caret to make additions. I tell my children that writers use carets to help them remember ideas. I explain that erasing takes longer and may cause a writer to forget ideas, particularly those ideas and words that were tough to sound-spell in the first place.

By asking the student to name the setting of a story, I frequently identify an area that needs expanding. I may focus a particular conference on reminding a child to include where and when the story takes place and to incorporate that new idea. We often choose a book with a similar setting from our Favorite Book Box to help us with the task.

By bringing examples of quality literature to our mini-lessons and writing conferences and focusing instruction on the features of excellent writing, young writers begin to view literature with a writer's eye. They also begin to listen with a writer's ear when others share their accomplishments in writing.

Adding Details

Matthew began first grade writing one-letter representations for words. By April, he had become a confident writer with easily read, complete stories. What follows is a sample of his work at the end of first grade. Matthew frequently used carets, or "carrot tops" as he calls them, to add details to his completed stories. His additions are in parentheses. We talked about including these details during our conference on story beginnings.

One (beautiful afternoon) day in a (lonely) cottage a (very nice) boy sat on a (nice) stair (really) thinking about a pair of (super) roller blades. One (magical) Friday, (super) roller blades appeared (magically) in the (living room) room. He tried them (super roller blades) on. The (super) roller blades just (magically) fell off his (nice) feet.

Matthew's Conference, Grade 1

Mrs. L.: Let's take a look at your beginning sentence.

Matthew: Okay, I wrote: "One day in a cottage a boy sat on a stair thinking about a pair of roller blades."

Mrs. L.: I know you are an expert on writing stories about roller blading, since you love to roller blade. I like your beginning sentence because I can picture the boy sitting on the stair. Is he outside of the cottage?

Matthew: Yes. I picture it being a sunny day.

Mrs. L.: I see. Is this first thing in the morning?

Matthew: No, it's afternoon.

Mrs. L.: How could we include this information in your story?

Matthew: I could add "One beautiful afternoon..."

Mrs. L.: That sounds like a great idea. Let's add those words with a "carrot top." What other words could we add to make the beginning more detailed?

Matthew: Well, he was a nice little boy and he was *really* thinking about those roller blades.

Mrs. L.: Let's fit these ideas into your story too. Tell me how we could do that.

Matthew: How about "a *very nice* boy sat on a *nice stair really* thinking about a pair of roller blades."

Mrs. L.: I like that. Read your sentence now.

Matthew: "One beautiful afternoon in a cottage"—I think I'll add *lonely* cottage—"a very nice boy sat on a nice stair really thinking about a pair of roller blades."

Mrs. L.: I think you have a detailed beginning now. You've told me where your story takes place—in a lonely cottage—and I have a nice picture of the setting in my mind.

Matthew: I think I want to say the boy was really thinking about super roller blades. And these roller blades will be magical!

Mrs. L.: That's a great idea!

Matthew: I'll put *super* beside roller blades.

Mrs. L.: Wow! Now your beginning sentence reads: "One beautiful afternoon in a lonely cottage, a very nice boy sat on a nice stair really thinking about a pair of super roller blades." I'm impressed with your detailed beginning, Matthew. Do you have ideas for continuing writing?

Matthew: I know I want the roller blades to magically appear in the living room the next day.

Mrs. L.: Okay, let's look at book that has magical things happening in it.

Matthew: *Sylvester and the Magic Pebble* might work. Sylvester wishes for something, and it happens.

Mrs. L.: Good thinking. Let's take a look...

Sylvester and the Magic Pebble by William Steig

Beginning Sentences

_____'s Beginning Sentences   Date _____

Self-Rating: _____

I st Try: _____

_____

2nd Try: _____

_____

Self-Rating: _____

I st Try: _____

_____

2nd Try: _____

_____

Self-Rating: _____

I st Try: _____

_____

2nd Try: _____

_____

Literature-Based Mini-Lessons to Teach Writing   Scholastic Professional Books

Books to Use:
Story Leads

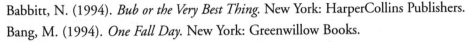

Babbitt, N. (1994). *Bub or the Very Best Thing*. New York: HarperCollins Publishers.

Bang, M. (1994). *One Fall Day*. New York: Greenwillow Books.

Brett, J. (1991). *Berlioz the Bear*. New York: G. P. Putnam's Sons.

———— (1987). *Goldilocks and the Three Bears*. New York: G. P. Putnam's Sons.

Brown, M. (1992). *Arthur Babysits*. Boston: Little, Brown and Company.

———— (1989). *Arthur's Birthday*. Boston: Little, Brown and Company.

———— (1986). *Arthur's Teacher Trouble*. Boston: Little, Brown and Company.

Calhoun, M. (1991). *High-Wire Henry*. New York: Morrow Junior Books.

Carle, E. (1969). *The Very Hungry Caterpillar*. New York: Philomel Books.

Ehlert, L. (1990). *Feathers for Lunch*. Orlando, Fl: Harcourt Brace Jovanovich.

Guarino, D. (1989). *Is Your Mama a Llama?* New York: Scholastic Inc.

Houston, G. (1992). *My Great-Aunt Arizona*. New York: HarperCollins Publishers.

Hest, A. (1984). *The Crack of Dawn Walkers*. New York: Macmillan Publishing Company.

———— (1993). *Nana's Birthday Party*. New York: Morrow Junior Books.

———— (1986). *The Purple Coat*. New York: Macmillan Publishing Company.

Ingman, B. (1995). *When Martha's Away*. Boston: Houghton Mifflin Company.

Isaacs, A. (1994). *Swamp Angel*. New York: Bantam Doubleday Dell Publishing Group, Inc.

Johnson, A. (1993). *Julius*. New York: Orchard Books.

Kellogg, S. (1986). *Best Friends*. New York: Dial Books for Young Readers.

———— (1996). *Yankee Doodle*. New York: Aladdin Paperbacks.

Kraus, R. (1971). *Leo the Late Bloomer*. New York: Harper and Row.

Mckissack, P. (1988). *Mirandy and Brother Wind*. New York: Bradbury Press.

Pilkey, D. (1993). *Dogzilla*. New York: Harcourt Brace & Company.

Polacco, P. (1993). *Babushka Baba Yaga*. New York: Philomel Books.

Rylant, C. (1982). *When I Was Young in the Mountains*. New York: E. P. Dutton.

Scieszka, J. (1991). *The Frog Prince Continued*. New York: Penguin Books.

Speed, T. (1995). *Two Cool Cows*. New York: G. P. Putnam's Sons.

Steig, W. (1976). *The Amazing Bone*. New York: Farrar Straus and Giroux.

———— (1969). *Sylvester and the Magic Pebble*. New York: Simon and Schuster.

Waber, B. (1987). *Funny, Funny Lyle*. Boston: Houghton Mifflin Company.

Wilson, G. (1994). *Prowlpuss*. Cambridge: Candlewick Press.

Yolen, J. (1987). *Owl Moon*. New York: Putnam Publishing Group.

Zion, G. (1956). *Harry the Dirty Dog*. New York: Harper and Row.

Using Descriptive Language

CHAPTER 4

The Mini-Lessons  The Writing Goals

The Mini-Lessons	The Writing Goals
The "Experts" Paint Pictures With Words	To develop an awareness of descriptive language used by "expert" authors
Working With Words	To paint pictures with words
Analogies: Take a Sentence—Make It Better	To explore analogies
Tired Words	To use descriptive words in place of commonly used words

Favorite Books to Use

Books that paint pictures with words, such as:

Night Tree by Eve Bunting

Owl Moon by Jane Yolen

The Polar Express by Chris Van Allsburg

The Purple Coat by Amy Hest

The Relatives Came by Cynthia Rylant

Seven Blind Mice by Ed Young

Stellaluna by Janelle Cannon

Books with rich vocabulary, such as:

The Amazing Bone by William Steig

Arthur's Teacher Trouble by Marc Brown

Chicken Little by Steven Kellogg

The "Experts" Paint Pictures With Words

GOAL To develop an awareness of the descriptive language used by "expert" authors

After I read a story to my students, we always talk about the catchy phrases, the illustrations, and the parts we liked best. It seems that the more we discuss a book, the more excited the children get about it. To bring this enthusiasm for books to our writers' workshop, I try to help my students capture the essence of what it is about certain books that makes us want to open them again and again. Our discussions teach the students to appreciate books and to talk about why they like particular books. When children are exposed to a variety of literature and allowed to explore their reading preferences, imitating the language from their favorite books comes naturally. Often these reading preferences lay the groundwork for a beginning writer's style.

Having children view literature with a writer's eye is critical for moving listeners who are aware of the reasons they love certain stories to become writers who attempt to include these qualities in their own writing. I'm always impressed and amazed by the descriptive language beginning writers are able to create as they learn to analyze the stories we read. Here's a mini-lesson that shows how we talk about language in books.

Mrs. L.: Remember at the beginning of the year when we were reading *The Relatives Came* by Cynthia Rylant, and you asked me to reread parts of the story? Tell me what you liked best.

Ryan: I like the part about "hugging time."

Mrs. L.: Let me find that page. We marked it: "You'd have to go through at least four different hugs to get from the kitchen to the front room." Even without the picture of the relatives hugging, you could see that picture in your mind. The words paint a picture of the hugging for us.

What else do you remember enjoying about this book?

Meghan: The part about new breathing.

Mrs. L.: We marked that page too. "It was different going to sleep with all that new breathing in the house." I can almost hear that new breathing. That reminds me of the page that says, "We crawled back into our beds that felt too big and too quiet."

Dana: That's my favorite page, even though it's sad.

Mrs. L.: Tell me about that page, Dana.

Dana: Well, the relatives left, and they miss the breathing now that they're gone. They miss the relatives.

Mrs. L.: I think you're right. Cynthia Rylant didn't have to write: "They missed the relatives." The "beds that felt too big and too quiet" paint a picture for us.

Let's look at some other favorite books that paint pictures with words. Painting pictures with words is a special quality that makes stories memorable. We can try to make our own stories extra special by learning how the experts paint pictures with words. Close your eyes for this one. Do you remember which story these sentences are from? "We ate candies with nougat centers as white as snow. We drank hot chocolate as thick and rich as melted chocolate bars."

Brett: *The Polar Express!*

Mrs. L.: You're right! Tell me what is special about those sentences.

Carrie: I could see that candy and hot chocolate when I had my eyes closed.

Mrs. L.: Chris Van Allsburg really paints a picture with his words, doesn't he?

Rebecca: I thought I could almost taste the hot chocolate.

Mrs. L.: Would this part of the sentence have been a favorite if he had written, "We drank good hot chocolate?"

Rebecca: No, I like "melted chocolate bars."

Mrs. L.: Me too. "Melted chocolate bars" is easy to imagine. Try this one. "She drags red-painted fingertips, slowly, across the rainbow of colors stacked in open shelves way up to the ceiling and down to the polished floor."

Lauren: *The Purple Coat.*

Mrs. L.: Yes! What makes this sentence special?

Lauren: If I close my eyes, I can see her hand choosing the color she wants for her new coat.

Carrie: Her red fingernails are easy to see.

Lauren: And the rainbow.

Mrs. L.: These details make the story special, don't they? Amy Hest could have written, "Gabby pointed to purple." What do you think about that sentence?

Amanda: It's boring. I like the words she really wrote.

Mrs. L.: Me too. Do you remember the part where Grampa shows Gabby the sandwiches? Some of you asked me to mark this page. "There's fun in Grampa's eyes. Magician-style, he uncovers a platter of sandwiches from the corner deli."

Katie: I like how she wrote "magician-style."

Mrs. L.: What if Amy Hest had written, "Grampa offered Gabby and her mother a sandwich?"

Katie: No! I like him pretending it's magic and pulling the cloth off the plate.

Mrs. L.: Me too. I also like the "fun in Grampa's eyes." Can you show me *fun* in your eyes? These sentences are special because they draw our

attention to the extra details happening in the story. These extra words make the story more exciting.

Stevie: We can see pictures in our minds without really seeing pictures in the book.

Mrs. L.: Yes, writers call this "painting pictures with words."

Tell me which sentences you remember from *Night Tree*. We marked lots of favorite pages in this book.

Dana: I like the first page, where they say going through the dark and quiet streets.

Mrs. L.: "We drive through the bright Christmas streets to where the dark and quiet begin."

Ellen: I guess it's "bright streets" because of the Christmas lights.

Brett: You know the lights wouldn't be as bright near the woods.

Dana: That's why it says "dark and quiet begin." I can see them driving away to the woods.

Sara: I like the part about the little girl jumping out of her boots.

Dana: Nina is the little girl.

Mrs. L.: Good remembering. Here's that page: "She hops up and down and right out of one of her boots." Tell me what you see when I read that sentence.

Ben: Nina is very happy. She reminds me of my little sister.

Mrs. L.: Eve Bunting didn't have to write "Nina was happy." She painted that picture with her words when Nina jumped up and down and out of her boot.

I like the page where she wrote, "There are secrets all around us." What do you think those secrets are?

Meghan: The owl is one secret. But you sort of have to picture in your mind what the other secrets are. I picture a bear and another deer watching from behind the trees.

Mrs. L.: Good ideas, Meghan. Any other favorite sentences?

Matthew: I like the part about his breath hurting.

Ben: It tells how cold it is.

Mrs. L.: "It's so cold my breath hurts."

Matthew: I've been that cold, and it does hurt to breathe.

Mrs. L.: I suppose writing "It was a very cold night" doesn't paint a great picture.

Matthew: No, and I like to kind of feel his breath hurting.

Mrs. L.: All of the books we shared today do an excellent job of painting pictures with words. How do you suppose these expert writers paint pictures with words?

Dana: I think they close their eyes and think really hard and write what they see.

Ben: I think they think of what they would see if they were in the story.

Katie: I think they practice writing lots of times until they get it right.

Mrs. L.: Yes, I bet authors do all of these things. Every author probably has his or her own way of painting pictures with words. You'll have to find your own way, too. Today during writing time, imagine yourself in your character's shoes. Write what the character is feeling, seeing, tasting, doing—and you will paint pictures with your words.

Remember, these writers have been using words in writing much longer than you. But if you practice and are not afraid to try new words, you might be surprised at what you write.

Extending the Mini-Lesson

STAR SENTENCES OF THE DAY

During another mini-lesson, we look at one of my drafts on the overhead. After identifying a simple sentence, "My cat was hungry," we decided to paint that picture with words by changing the sentence to "M-e-o-w-m-e-o-w-M-E-O-W. Chanti the cat sat next to her bowl, begging for breakfast." The students were eager to share their favorite written sentences. I asked them to put a star beside such sentences. When I announce that writing time is over for a particular day, I ask for "star sentences of the day," and we share these sentences that paint pictures. This makes better use of our sharing time by allowing us to hear descriptive language without taking time to share an entire story. I reserve a page in my notebook for the students' sentences that paint pictures, and I display them on a chart.

Star Sentences

- One nice spring day I was walking down the green grass path. (Tracie)

- The boy went outside to fly his purple kite when all of a sudden, a strong wind came along and blew the kite out of his hand. (Joe)

- The black and white ball went flying down to the other end of enormous soccer field. (Kristen)

- So, I trotted down the winding path with the baby Triceratops running beside me. (Meghan)

- The ocean has some interesting pretty and colorful seashells if you look for them early in the morning. (Colleen)

MECHANICS: CAPITALS, PERIODS, AND QUESTION MARKS

My second-grade writers need exposure to the proper use of capital letters and ending punctuation. And this skill doesn't become automatic for beginning writers without lots of practice. Occasionally during a mini-lesson on one of our favorite books, I'll copy a few sentences on an overhead transparency or the board without the capitals and periods. I then proceed to read my newly found treasured sentences as if nothing is wrong:

> on summer days they warmed their old bones together in the sun on fall days they took long walks through the trees and on winter days they turned the opera up very loud after a while it seemed as if they had always lived together

Mr. Putter and Tabby Pour the Tea by Cynthia Rylant

The students are quick to notice that my copied sentences lack punctuation. Together we add the missing periods. Then we change the first letter of each sentence to a capital. During the editing stage, I remind my students to add capitals and periods to their own writing efforts.

On another day, we use the book *Backstage With Clawdio* by Harriet Berg Schwartz to talk about the use of question marks. After a brief discussion of asking and telling sentences, we add the missing periods or question marks.

> Then I move on to the front of the theater __ Have the street doors been unlocked__ Are there stacks of programs for tonight's performance__ Are the ushers at their stations__ Backstage again, I peep from behind the curtain to watch the audience take their seats__

FAVORITE BOOKS

Following our read-aloud selections, the children and I continue to discuss sentences that paint pictures with words. The children had seen me mark the pages of our favorite parts of stories with sticky notes; soon, they were borrowing sticky notes to mark places of their own. This was a natural extension of our first mini-lesson on descriptive language and a habit that wasn't limited to writers' workshop or read-aloud but continued throughout the school day. During silent reading time, hands were often raised to share a favorite sentence. I became aware of the children's growing appreciation for an author's use of descriptive language and watched with excitement as they began to imitate this technique in their own writing efforts. I became convinced that the authors of children's literature were making a positive impact on our writers' workshop.

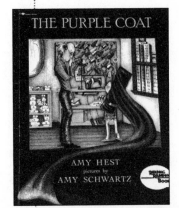

A "Favorite Book" chosen for sharing

MAKING THE MOST OF EXTRA MINUTES

The results of the children's writing efforts may not be as sophisticated as those of Rylant or Van Allsburg, but after our mini-lessons on descriptive language, I see more risk-taking and comfort in writing. I also see a desire to share favorite descriptive language, both from the literature they read and from what they write. Our time spent waiting in line for lunch or art becomes time spent reading sentences the students changed for more details. Stephanie's "We had fun" became "We laughed and played for hours." Taylor's "friendly" dinosaur became a dinosaur that "held my hand."

As I watch children's faces during these impromptu sharing times, I realize they're listening closely. Many of the ideas show up in later writings of other students. As Temple et al. note in *The Beginnings of Writing:* "Children find resources for composing in the stories they hear and read—and not just stories but other catchy uses of language, too."

Developing a Literary Style

One day, when we met on the carpet for sharing time, Allie shared changes in a story she had written called "Fritz and the Messy Room," based on Rosemary Wells' book Fritz and the Mess Fairy. She began:

"Fritz, go clean your room." "O.K., Mom." He pushed seventeen empty stinky chocolate milk glasses under his bed and ten empty ice cream bowls and threw the rest of his toys in the closet. "I'm done!" Fritz screamed...

Allie's First Draft

Allie Adds Descriptive Language

Originally, Allie had mom discovering the messy closet when "Mom went to put the new closet door on" and telling Fritz to "clean up the room for real." Allie changed the story to add details of what happened when Mom discovered the mess. Allie cut a strip of paper, glued it to the top of her draft, and wrote:

(Then Mom *went to put the new)* closet door on. She was buried in toys. Then she yelled, "Fritz you get up here this minute or else. Fritz, where are you?" Fritz did not come. Fritz was hiding in the backyard behind some bushes. He bit his nails. Fritz always bit his nails when he was scared. He heard his mother tramping up the steps. He got even "scareder." He had a shiver down his back...

Allie's stories have the cadence and rhythm of the experts' stories, a noteworthy accomplishment for a 7-year-old. She's the kind of student who hangs on to every word during read-aloud time. As I read her stories, I realized she stored the phrases and ideas of the experts to apply them to her own creations. Although Allie was one of the first writers to develop a literary style, many others began to make dramatic changes in their writing efforts as well. These young writers began thinking, researching, and writing like the experts. My role as a teacher was to "be aware of those moments when students create powerful images of their own, when they use language to boldly extend their thinking." (*What a Writer Needs*, by Ralph Fletcher; Heinemann, 1993)

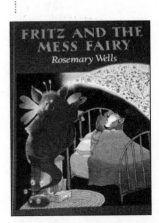

Fritz and the Mess Fairy
by Rosemary Wells

Working With Words

GOAL To paint pictures with words

We begin using the idea of "painting pictures with words" when we discuss the book If You Were a Writer. *Joan Lowery Nixon's character explains how "a writer works with words." She says, "If you were a writer, you would think of words that make pictures." This idea sets the stage for a yearlong writers' workshop goal. "Painting pictures with words" is a great descriptive phrase, just like the models we find in the best works of children's literature. It is also an effective phrase to use with young writers who are just beginning to include descriptive language in their stories.*

The previous mini-lesson, "The Experts Paint Pictures With Words," begins to build an awareness of the kinds of sentences that paint pictures. Next, students are ready to take a look at how the authors perform such magic, how they feel what is happening in a story. A beginning "hands-on" approach shows the students that painting pictures with words isn't as difficult as it may appear. They're eager to do more work with words after the following mini-lesson.

BEFORE WE BEGIN

In a bag, I place objects that could be described with "words that paint pictures," such as a wool mitten, a lemon or apple, cookies (or candy, one per student), a silky piece of fabric, a brush, costume jewelry, a small box wrapped in birthday paper, and a small teddy bear.

Mrs. L.: Today we're going to be working with words like we do every day during writers' workshop. But this time, we're going to concentrate on those words that help us paint a picture. Remember in the story *If You Were a Writer*, Melia's mother said, "a writer works with words. If you were a writer, you would think of words that make pictures." Today we'll think of words that make pictures of the objects in this bag.

I'm going to choose the first two objects, but I'll be asking for your help with the rest. I put these first two objects in the bag because they're like things Melia painted pictures of with her words.

Maggie: I remember when she smelled the apple pie.

Tracie: That part made me hungry.

Mrs. L.: That part made many of us hungry! I want to start with this piece of fabric. It's just like the fabric Melia felt when she touched her mother's arm and said, "the words slippery, slithery, and soft slid into her mind." I will record your words that paint pictures on the board while you take turns holding each object.

Rebecca: *Cool...and smooth.*

Mrs. L.: Good words. I'll write them on the board.

Lauren:	I have a great word—*satiny*—like my ballet shoes.
Mrs. L.:	Great! We could paint a picture of the mother's blouse with the words *cool*, *smooth*, and *satiny*. Here's my second object—a hairbrush. I put this in here to remind you of something else Melia described in the book.
Matthew:	Her dad's beard?
Mrs. L.:	Close, it was Uncle John's "whiskery mustache." I marked the page in the book. "Melia ran to hug him, and the words *bristly* and *bushy* bounced into her thoughts." Pass the brush around, and let's think of other words that paint a picture of this bristly, bushy hairbrush or mustache.
Brett:	*Sharp.*
Carrie:	*Pointy.*
Stevie:	*Rough and jagged.*
Mrs. L.:	Excellent words. We could paint a picture of the mustache with the words *sharp*, *pointy*, *rough*, *bristly*, *bushy*, and *jagged*.
	Matthew, would you please choose another object from the bag?
Matthew:	It's a lemon.
Dana:	*Sour* is a word for sure!
Ellen:	*Yellow.*
Lauren:	How about *sun-yellow*?
Rebecca:	If I tasted it, I would say it's *tart* and *bitey*.
Katie:	*Lip-puckering.*
Mrs. L.:	What good describing words! You're great at painting pictures with words.
	Ellen, would you like to choose an object from the bag?
Ellen:	Sure...it's a pretend ring.
Stephanie:	*Sparkly...glittery.*
Ryan:	*Clear red.*
Meghan:	No, *ruby-red*.
Sara:	*Glassy.*
Katie:	I have a good one. *Dazzling.*
Mrs. L.:	All these words are helpful for painting a picture of the ring. The ring is *sparkly*, *glittery*, *clear ruby-red*, *glassy*, and *dazzling*. Wow!
Ben:	Anything else in the bag?
Mrs. L.:	Why don't you check, Ben.
Ben:	A present. A birthday present. I can tell from the paper.
Kristen:	*Mysterious* is a word to use because we don't know what's inside.
Samuel:	*Small.*
Tommy:	*New?* Because most presents are new things.
Mrs. L.:	Sure.
Amanda:	*Cheerful and brightly wrapped.*
Mrs. L.:	How would you like to get a small, new, mysterious, brightly-wrapped-in-cheerful-paper birthday present?
Ryan:	Can we open it?

Mrs. L.: The tag says for Mrs. C. so we'd better not. Let's look in the bag for something else.

Brett: I picked a teddy bear. He's fuzzy...and soft.

Carrie: Lovable.

Sara: Tan-brown.

Stephanie: Cuddly.

Meghan: So cute you want to hug him.

Amanda: I think he looks shy.

Mrs. L.: Once again, you've come up with some great words. Would *bristly* work for this bear?

Stevie: No. He's very soft.

Mrs. L.: Smile if you have a fuzzy, soft, lovable, tan-brown cuddly, shy bear who is so cute you want to hug him. I'm picturing my bear sitting on my bed right now. Your turn to choose, Ryan.

Ryan: Yum—chocolate-chip cookies.

Class: Mmmmm...

Ryan: I think they look homemade.

Mrs. L.: No, they're from a supermarket bakery. So, how could we describe them?

Meghan: *Soft* like homemade. *Not crunchy* like some store-bought cookies.

Tommy: How about *from a supermarket bakery.*

Amanda: Or *just like homemade.*

Mrs. L.: Good ideas. What else?

David: Crumbly.

Ben: Sweet.

Ellen: Delicious because of the chocolate chips.

Lauren: Melt-in-your-mouth chocolate chips.

Ben: I'm getting hungry...

Mrs. L.: Raise your hand if you would like to taste a just-like-homemade, soft-not-crunchy, crumbly, sweet, delicious chocolate chip cookie. Looks unanimous. I know there are enough for everyone. I'll pass them out while you taste-test and practice painting pictures with the words in your stories.

"Painting Pictures With Words"

Taste-testing crumbly chocolate chip cookies

Extending the Mini-Lesson

TELL ME MORE

We continue to practice painting pictures with words whenever we come across an unusual object. For example, I may ask: "What words pop into your mind when you touch this pussy willow branch?" At times, we extend this idea to painting pictures of feelings: "Tell me how you'd feel if somebody bumped you off the swing" or "Tell me how you felt on the first day of school." Sometimes our mini-lesson involves taking five minutes to jot down responses to a tell-me statement and then sharing those responses. As we practice painting pictures with words and sharing ideas, the students become more comfortable working with their own words on paper. After hearing Lois Ehlert's story, *Nuts to You*, Sara wrote a story about the time she woke up to find a chipmunk outside her window:

One breezy fall day when I woke up, I hurried out of my bed and I heard a noise—Peep, Peep. It was a chipmunk. It was near a leaf. I got it a nice warm blanket. I found...

Although Sara used simple sentences, the words "near a leaf" help to paint a picture of the chipmunk's surroundings.

MISSING DETAILS

By modeling appropriate questions after story sharing time, students begin to anticipate missing details. One day, Ben wrote a story about getting two coins from the tooth fairy. My job was to ask, "What kind of coins?" When Ben added "shiny" to his sentence, he illustrated a simple way to work with words in a story that he later titled "Two Shiny Coins."

This questioning technique is effective for extending the sentences of beginning writers. Sara's story about a birthday party ended rather simply: "We ate cake and went home." After I asked, "What kind of cake?," her ending changed to: "We ate chocolate cake with chocolate icing and pink sprinkles. Then we went home."

USING DIALOGUE

Since dialogue makes stories more detailed by showing character interactions, another good extension activity for descriptive language is a mini-lesson that introduces conversation. Using the book *Martha Calling*, I copy a page in my own words on the board, without using dialogue.

> "They went for a swim. Then they played a game of Ping-Pong. They had a nice picnic lunch. It was fun. But Martha couldn't go."

Beside this, I copy the same page as it was written, with dialogue:

> "Let's go for a swim," said Father.
> "Then we can have a game of Ping-Pong," said Helen.
> "And a nice picnic lunch," added Mother.
> "Sounds like fun," said Martha.
> But mother said, "Sorry, Martha."
> "I'll sneak you out after dark," said Helen.

We discuss how dialogue makes the story more exciting and more natural by having the characters talk back and forth, as it would happen in real life. On another day, we use the book *Somebody and Three Blairs* to further show the effectiveness of dialogue. I ask the students to tell which page they prefer:

> It was a fine morning. Mr. Blair, Mrs. Blair, and Baby Blair went for a walk in the park. It was a good idea. So they took their coats and a bag of bread crumbs and set out for the park.

or

> "It's such a fine morning," said Mr. Blair.
> "Let's take a walk in the park."
> "What a good idea," said Mrs. Blair.
> "Feeda ducks," said Baby Blair.
> So they took their coats and a bag of bread and set out for the park.

The students agree that "feeda ducks" makes the story more exciting and that without conversation, this great idea is lost. Together, we edit some student stories to include dialogue. Using conversation is often a beginning writer's first attempt at writing more complex sentences.

Before our mini-lesson on dialogue, Stephanie had been working on a story called "Baby Dinosaurs." After the mini-lesson, she sat down with another sheet of paper and began recopying her story to include a conversation between herself and her brother Nicholas. The first version, which included basic "telling" sentences, was placed in the recyling container when her sharing group told her how much they liked having her argue with Nicholas about the danger these dinosaurs posed.

> Baby Dinosaurs
> One day. I was working on my homework
> and all a sudin it felt like a earthquake
> was at our house. So I looked out my
> window and it turned into what it looked
> like when the dinosaurs were a live with
> only baby dinosaurs. Cool said Nicholas my
> brother. I said oh no. Nicholas this
> is not cool this is dangeris. No they arn't
> said Nicholas yes they "I said sort of
> mad. They could hurt us or kill us. Ahm
> mahmmmm! said Nicholas. It's
> true Nicholas I said. Only ten of the

> Will not hurt us or kill us. So we
> can keep the riht kinds of dinosaurs
> for a pet into it's to big. But then we
> can visit it when ever we want. The ones
> that that are nice frindly and funny
> like the Long neck and the other ones
> that have a long neck like the
> Brontosaurus Dipladocus and the others
> with long necks if ther is?

PICTURES WORK WITH WORDS

Beginning writers often include the details in their pictures but forget to add these words to the story. Encouraging the writer to include at least one detail from the picture often gets the ball rolling for more descriptive sentences. You can ask less able writers to dictate details, using their illustrations for guidance.

MORE COMPLEX SENTENCES

I hold a writing conference or mini-lesson with a small group of more able writers and use the book *Stellaluna* to show how *-ing* words are used as describing words. I read the following sentences, and we discuss how the *-ing* words show extra details.

Dodging and *shrieking,* Mother Bat tried to escape, but the owl struck again and again, knocking Stellaluna into the air.

and

Wrapping her wings about her, she clutched the thin branch, *trembling* with cold and fear.

Together, we search the Favorite Books Box to find other examples of *-ing* words that add details. Then students share their discoveries during a future sharing time, letting their fellow writers in on another secret of the "experts."

One quiet afternoon at the world of Puppy Land, Pup-u-Roo was admiring his shimmering purple jewel when someone came knocking at his door...

> One quiet afternoon
> at the world of pappy
> Land pup-u-roo was
> admireing his shimreing
> Purple jale someone
> came knoking on his door

77

Analogies: Take a Sentence— Make It Better!

GOAL To explore analogies

*T*he Polar Express *inspired the following mini-lesson. Van Allsburg's use of analogies—as big as, as thick as, as fast as—is a simple but effective descriptive language technique to use with beginning writers. Since children often use analogies in their oral language, I remind my writers that "if you can say it, you can write it." I begin with simple color analogies to get students thinking about our mini-lesson goal. I list these on the board as we begin our writers' meeting.*

Mrs. L.: Please join me on the carpet if you are wearing a color as:

blue as the summer sky.

orange as a Halloween pumpkin.

red as a ripe juicy apple.

yellow as a tall glass of lemonade.

pink as a piglet.

(I continue naming colors until all children are called.)

Mrs. L.: During our last writers' meeting, we talked about the special way authors paint pictures with words. Today we'll learn another way authors make sentences even better, a different way to paint pictures with words. I think you will be surprised at how easy it can be to give your audience details about what is happening in your story.

I called you back to our meeting today using color details. I helped you paint a clearer picture in your minds with words like "pink as a piglet."

Tommy: That made it more fun.

Mrs. L.: I agree. How did I paint a picture of these colors with my words?

Meghan: You said the color and you compared something that is that color. My color was red as a juicy apple.

Mrs. L.: When writers take something you know about—like melted chocolate bars—and compare it to something you may not know about—like how thick—it helps the reader to get a better picture of what is happening in the story. Authors often use the word *as* to compare what we know with what the writer wants us to understand. For example, when Chris Van Allsburg wrote "We drank hot cocoa as thick and rich as melted chocolate bars" in *The Polar Express*, he helped us understand just how thick the hot cocoa really is.

Samuel: The kids on the Polar Express ate candy like snow too.

Mrs. L.: You're right. That sentence paints a picture of what the center of the candy looks like: "...and ate candy with nougat centers *as* white *as* snow."

Ed Young is another expert on writing details to help readers understand what is happening in the story. I'm going to reread one of our favorite books, *Seven Blind Mice*. Listen for other sentences that use the "as _____ as _____" idea to give more details.

(We reread *Seven Blind Mice*. When we reached the page that White Mouse sees "The Something," the class stopped me.)

Class: Stop!

Robbie: Those are detail words.

Stephanie: The "as sharp as a spear" words.

Mrs. L.: Great! Let's reread the *as* _____ *as* _____ words:

> as sturdy as a pillar,
>
> supple as a snake,
>
> wide as a cliff,
>
> sharp as a spear,
>
> breezy as a fan,
>
> stringy as a rope.

What do you think of these words?

Stephanie: I like "breezy as a fan" and "stringy as a rope." I picture a fan and a rope. The elephant's tail is the rope.

Mrs. L.: You're right. What was breezy as a fan?

Carrie: His ear.

Mrs. L.: Good! Did Ed Young help you see what each mouse saw when he or she went to the pond?

Stevie: Yes, the other mice go one at a time. So each mouse needs to use something the other mice have seen before so that they can get a picture of what the mouse saw when she was by herself at the pond.

Mrs. L.: Exactly. When an author wants the audience to see or feel or hear or taste something that he may not have experienced before, he has to compare it to something the reader has experienced. This is called an *analogy*. It's a special technique writers use to help them paint pictures with words. It's easy to do, and it makes a story detailed. Let me share some other analogies from other favorite books.

	In the Christmas story, *Night Tree*, Eve Bunting uses an analogy to describe the moon. Let me read that sentence.
Ryan:	She says the moon's big as a basketball.
Mrs. L.:	How did you remember?
Ryan:	I like basketball, and I remember when you read it thinking the moon does sometimes look like a yellow-white basketball.
David:	Only when it's a full moon.
Mrs. L.:	Good thinking. That's what makes analogies fun to read and write. You write details to help your audience know exactly what you're picturing in your mind when you write a particular sentence. Eve Bunting wrote: "The sky is spattered with stars, and the moon, *big as a basketball*, slides in and out between the treetops."
Dana:	I like that sentence.
Lauren:	I like "slides in and out between the treetops."
Tommy:	I like "big as a basketball."
Mrs. L.:	Here's another favorite of mine. In *Owl Moon*, Jane Yolen uses analogies to help us understand what the winter night was like by comparing the characters' experiences to things we have probably experienced too.
	When the dogs were barking and stopped, she wrote: "And when their voices faded away it was *as quiet as a dream*."
Sara:	Dreams are quiet—unless they're nightmares.
Mrs. L.:	Do you know just how quiet the night must have been?
Meghan:	Yes, dream quiet.
Mrs. L.:	Close your eyes and imagine "dream quiet..." Here's another analogy later in the story when Jane Yolen is trying to describe the moon. "It seemed to fit exactly over the center of the clearing and the snow below it was *whiter than the milk in a cereal bowl*."
	You know how white milk is, so you could imagine how white the snow must have been.
David:	Not black like snow on the road.
Mrs. L.:	We talked earlier about the candy with centers as white as snow. Why do you think authors write "white as snow"?
Amanda:	Probably because everybody knows how white snow is.
Mrs. L.:	Good thinking! There's another analogy in *The Polar Express* that uses the moon. Here's the analogy: "We climbed mountains so high it seemed as if we would scrape the moon." This time we're picturing *as high as the moon*. In *Owl Moon*, Jane Yolen was writing about *as round as the moon*.
	I have a sentence in my story that would be good for an analogy because I'm talking about the color of my dog, Sydney. Please help me improve this sentence of my draft that tells: "Sydney is a brown dog." Do these words help you get a picture of the color brown?
Ellen:	No, lots of dogs are brown and they are all different colors of brown.

80

Mrs. L.: You're right. Sydney is a certain shade of brown, and when I see that color of brown it makes me think of ...

Samuel: Chocolate bars—she's a chocolate lab.

Mrs. L.: So tell me what to write to give my audience a better picture of Sydney.

Samuel: Sydney is as brown as a Hershey's chocolate bar.

Rebecca: Or a bowl of unwrapped chocolate kisses.

Mrs. L.: Both of these ideas paint a better picture of brown. The reader doesn't have to guess what color of brown Sydney is or even look at the picture in my story. My words give the details.

Let's try to write a few analogies together. I've written the beginning of some analogies on chart paper. You can help me finish the sentences:

> as tall as...
>
> as skinny as ...
>
> as happy as...
>
> as hungry as...
>
> as prickly as...
>
> as sad as...

I think you'll agree that writing analogies is a fun way for writers to paint pictures with words. It's easy, too. Just close your eyes and imagine something that will help your readers paint a picture in their minds...

We write the first volunteer's idea on the chart. Together, we 'brainstorm,' discussing the endless possibilities for completing each analogy. After our mini-lesson, our chart looked like this:

> as tall as a skyscraper that touched the moon
>
> as skinny as a piece of paper
>
> as happy as a kid on Christmas
>
> as hungry as a starving dinosaur
>
> as prickly as a cactus
>
> as sad as a puppy who got in trouble for chewing a shoe

Then I add one last analogy of my own:

> as happy as a teacher with great writers like you

The children's analogies show them that taking a familiar object and comparing it to something else in an unusual way helps make their writing more meaningful. Using analogies gives beginning writers a simple, effective way to move from basic sentence writing to a more complex form of writing. Most of the children find analogies a fun challenge and eagerly include them in the stories they write during writing time.

Extending the Mini-Lesson

ANALOGIES CHART

Soon after this initial mini-lesson on analogies, we add another page to our class flip-chart. This page displays analogies from the experts and our own classroom writers. The students are often surprised to learn that particular analogies were written by fellow writers, not the "expert" authors we invite to our writers' workshop mini-lessons. We continue to talk about comparing sentences, identifying sentences in the students' work that could be made into analogies, and identifying analogies from books we share during read-aloud.

Analogies

- The sky is spattered with stars, and the moon, <u>big as a basketball</u>, slides in and out between the treetops.
  (Night Tree, Bunting)

- The eyes were <u>as gray as a rain cloud</u>. (Tracie, Grade 2)

- And when their voices faded away it was <u>as quiet as a dream.</u>
  (Owl Moon, Yolen)

- Her hands were <u>as brown as dirt.</u> (Stephanie, Grade 2)

- I ran almost as quick <u>as a train going down the track.</u>
  (Allisa, Grade 1)

- We climbed mountains so high it seemed <u>as if we would scrape the moon.</u> (The Polar Express, Van Allsburg)

- His shirt was <u>white like a cloud on a sunny day.</u> (John, Grade 1)

TEAMWORK

During another mini-lesson, we work in teams to finish analogy starters. I gave each group a copy of five analogy starters to complete. (See the form at the end of this chapter.)

as scared as...   as little as...   as purple as...
as itchy as...   as wet as...

We share our completed lists and are surprised by the results.

Concrete analogies, using color, size, and shape, are easier for some children. Eventually, I ask the students to think about feelings (*as scared as..., as happy as...*) to broaden their understanding of the possibilities for analogies. Knowing that everyone may imagine a different shade when the color purple is mentioned helps students see the need for using analogies. Knowing there is not a single answer to this task makes students enjoy analogies even more.

Our Analogies

as scared as a prison Falling off a very big moontain

as little as a Teenemite

as purple as a plum

as itchy as chicken poxs

as wet as water

Our Analogies

as scared as a Kid when he has a Baddrean

as little as an ant

as purple as Purple grape Juice.

as itchy as you when you have Chiken pocs

as wet as you When you get out of the Bath tub

Randy Uses Descriptive Language

Randy had spent the first eight months of first grade using illustrations and verbal descriptions to tell his stories, because his fine-motor skills made letter formation difficult. While we worked on improving these skills through drawing and letter practice, I encouraged his oral story telling. And I was thrilled when he made his first attempt at using descriptive language to tell a story.

I had asked him to tell me about a picture he'd drawn, and he said, "The gold is as orange as the sunset..." I pleaded with Randy to put his crayons down long enough to write that one sentence under his picture. He put as much into writing his words as he had always put into drawing his pictures. As his fine-motor skills improve, I believe his stories will be full of the rich vocabulary that he has read or heard in children's literature and that he so confidently speaks.

The gold is <u>as orange as sunset</u>.

this Gol Is orange as sunset

Tired Words

GOAL To use descriptive words in place of commonly used words

When my students begin using conversation in their stories, I'm thrilled to see the transition from simple to more complex sentence writing. But then I see a familiar pattern of simple words being used over and over again: "He said," "I said," or "Then I said" begin or end nearly every sentence. Now I know it's time to demonstrate how to replace these "tired" words.

Mrs. L.: Today we're going look at another challenge writers face—the challenge of using different words instead of the same tired words over and over and over again. I call these "tired" words because the reader gets tired of reading them. Our language is filled with great words, and as writers, we should explore using many different words—not just the same old tired words.

Today I'm going to reread Steven Kellogg's version of *Chicken Little*, because I am impressed with the many different words he used in place of the word *said*. *Said* is a tired word, and there are many other words that paint a clearer picture of *how* the character is saying something.

As I'm reading, you listen for a word that means "said." Say "stop" when you hear one of those words. I'll quickly write that word on the board. When we're finished, we'll count the number of different words that mean the same or almost the same as *said*.

(I reread the story, pausing to write the synonyms for said.)

Chicken Little Said ...

announced (3)	cried(5)	whispered	declared
chuckled(2)	observed	murmured	sneered
shrieked (2)	demanded	chorused	snapped
asked	wailed	added	squawked

David: Wow! 16 ways!

Tommy: And he never said *said* once!

Mrs. L.: Tell me how you think Steven Kellogg did this.

Tommy: Well, he used better words than just *said*. *Squawked* sounds better than *said*.

Mrs. L.:   I agree. Any other thoughts?

Dana: Well, *snapped* tells more about the story. *Snapped* means mad...not like you snapped your fingers.

Mrs. L.:   So you know to read that part in a mad voice.

'You mean I'm under a fat hippo,' snapped Foxy Loxy."

(I read this in a mad voice)

Stevie: Yes, if he wrote *said*, you'd read the sentence in a plain voice.

Mrs. L.:   I see. Tell me why you think Steven Kellogg used the word *cried* five times.

Dana: Well, for one thing, if he wrote *said* 16 times it would get boring.

Mrs. L.:   It just might. Any other ideas?

Stephanie: Well, I think the story was about how scared they were when the sky was falling, so they didn't just say it, they *cried* it.

Mrs. L.:   Let's give it a try. *Cry* out: "the sky is falling."

Class: THE SKY IS FALLING!

Mrs. L.:   Great, now say: "the sky is falling."

Class: The sky is falling.

Mrs. L.:   What a difference! The words Steven Kellogg wrote helped him paint a picture of his story and let the reader know more details about the character's feelings.

Let's try doing this with the other words on the list. You repeat "the sky is falling" each time I point to one of Steven Kellogg's words.

Ready?

Announce that the sky is falling (students announce).

Chuckle the sky is falling (students chuckle).

Shriek ...

Ask if...

Observe...

(We continue with the rest of the words on the list, stopping when necessary for a brief vocabulary lesson).

Mrs. L.:   There are many tired words. If you find yourself using the same word over and over again, try to step into your story and think of a new way of writing that word. You might *stumble* instead of *walk*, *giggle* instead of *laugh*, or *munch* instead of *eat*. Your story will be more exciting, and you just might have more fun writing it.

FIRST-GRADE AUTHOR: ▶

We went outside. There was an elevator. "We're saved!" I <u>announced</u>. "Not quite," Aileen <u>cried</u>. "Neah," she <u>added</u>, "Let's go check it out." When we got to the...

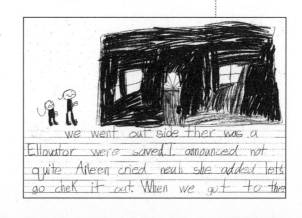

Extending the Lesson

OTHER BOOKS TO USE

We continue to add words to our list of "said" words after read-aloud. When we read Marc Brown's *Arthur's Teacher Trouble*, the words *warned, shouted, cheered, grumbled, called, continued, added, answered,* and *repeated* become part of our list. *Replied, commanded, growled, screamed, (breathlessly) exclaimed, whimpered, yelled, laughed, snarled, sobbed, sighed, intoned, ordered,* and *remarked* are added after we share Steig's *The Amazing Bone.*

STUDENT THESAURUSES

My friend and fellow teacher, Cindy Cowan, thought of the following activity for making individual student thesauruses. The students label the pages of a composition book from A to Z. Together, we brainstorm a list of synonyms for a particular "tired" word. Students copy at least 10 words from the list into their thesauruses, which they keep in their writing folders to use when they're editing a story.

Occasionally, the primary teachers in our school cooperate in a thesaurus-word contest. The teachers choose a particular word and see which class generates the most synonyms for it. This healthy competition gives the lesson an added challenge and creates more possibilities for replacing overused words.

S	Said
1 announced	10 Whispered
2 Shrieked	11 nodded
3 Obseved	12 snapped
4 Wailed	13 Cried
5 Chorused	14 Squacked
6 Scaremed	15 Murmured
7 Chuckled	16 declared
8 asked	17 Sneered
9 demaanded	

Sample of a thesaurus page

ARTIST CHAT

Following our lesson on Steven Kellogg's *Chicken Little,* I share a section of the book *Talking With Artists,* compiled and edited by Pat Cummings (Simon & Schuster, 1992). I read the section on Steven Kellogg, and we spend a mini-lesson talking about Steven Kellogg as an illustrator. The students enjoy seeing a sample of Steven Kellogg's childhood drawings and listening to where his ideas originate. This mini-lesson shows the young artists in the class that it's possible to grow up and have a job that includes a love of drawing.

A young artist's inspiration: <u>Chrysanthemum</u> *by Kevin Henkes*

The Writing Conference

ANECDOTAL RECORDS

I keep records of progress relating to descriptive language on a separate page in my writing notebook labeled "Sentences That Paint Pictures." As I come across a student's sentence that includes descriptive language, I record it along with the student's name and date. I also chart a list of these sentences to stimulate others to write similar sentences.

Sentences That Paint Pictures:

- The sun was as warm as a bowl of oatmeal. —Rebecca, Jan. 12

- I raced down the street as fast as my legs would go. —Stevie, Jan. 24

- My new shoes were shiny like a new penny. —Dana, Feb. 3

As I meet with individual students, I locate a sentence in the story that could be edited for descriptive language. Together, we add analogies, exchange tired words for better details, and look to our Favorite Books Box for assistance.

BROWSING THROUGH THE BOOK BOX

Often during a conference, the student and I browse through a book by an author who has written a story similar in topic or feeling to the student's work. We reread certain pages, talking about what it is that makes a particular story pleasant to read. Together, we research as "real" writers do, looking for ways to edit the student's stories to make them better. This modeling fosters an awareness of descriptive language and helps students realize why they like certain kinds of books and stories. Often, this preference influences the child's own writing.

Two writers share a book from the Favorite Books Box

GROUP CONFERENCES

Usually about the time we begin exploring descriptive language, certain students begin developing a style of writing. Some are mimicking a particular writer's style, while others seem to be adept at using rich vocabulary words following lessons on tired words. When styles of writing become apparent, I group students for conferences to provide direct instruction that reaches their needs as developing writers. Conferences with writers who are at a similar level and working on similar skills help to extend learning.

Helping Advanced Students

When I realized that Lauren and Katie's styles had begun to blossom after reading *The Purple Coat*, it made sense to pull them together to expand their use of words that paint pictures. Lauren and Katie, strong second-grade writers who were using complex sentences, were ready for advanced writing techniques. The three of us spent time during a writing conference to further explore Amy Hest's use of descriptive language.

Lauren and Katie's Conference:

Mrs. L.: After I read your stories "The Tangerine Coat" and "The Jelly-Bean Black Coat," I thought the three of us should take a closer look at Amy Hest's book, *The Purple Coat*. You're both writing spinoffs of her story. What else do you remember liking about this story?

Lauren: I like the sentence where she pulls her sock up and takes her foot out of her shoe.

Katie: That's the part when her mom says she should get a navy coat.

Mrs. L.: Let's look at that page.
What do these words tell you about how Gabby is feeling?

Katie: It shows she's disappointed and really wants a purple coat.

Mrs. L.: This is a technique expert writers often use. They *show* what is happening instead of *tell* what is happening. Amy Hest never had to write "Gabby was sad." She showed you Gabby was upset by the way she slid her shoe in and out of her moccasin.

Lauren: I like it better this way.

Katie: I see it better in my mind.

Mrs. L.: I agree. These words make a better picture.
How else could you show that a character is upset?

Katie: Well, when I'm upset sometimes I stomp my feet.

Lauren: I do that when I'm mad. When I'm sad, I sometimes cry.

Mrs. L.: Do you ever bite your lip to keep from crying?

Katie: Not hard, but like this (she bites her lip).

Mrs. L.: So we could write something like "Mom said navy coats are best. Gabby bit her lip..."

Katie: To stop the tears.

Lauren: Or, to keep from arguing with her mom. I do that sometimes.

Mrs. L.: There are times when we all should bite our lips to keep certain words inside! I wrote a story once about an argument I had with my

brother when I was in kindergarten. I remember writing "a teardrop bounced off my sneaker. I kicked it away."

Katie: I remember when you read that story to us.

Mrs. L.: I wonder if there are any sentences in your stories that we could *show* instead of *tell* what's happening—to paint a better picture with our words. Let's take a look...

AFTER REVISION, KATIE'S SENTENCE BECAME:

Grandpa was pacing around with his black tailored suit on.

> *Granpa was pasing arawnd whith his black taler sut on.*

AFTER REVISION, LAUREN'S SENTENCE BECAME:

Vanessa sighed as they walked down the city streets. "Why can't I get a tangerine coat?" said Vanessa with another sigh.

> *Vanessa side as thay wold down the city streets Wiy cant I get a tangerine coat? said Vanessa with another siy*

Lauren's story illustration

Group's Name _____

Our Analogies

as scared as _____

as little as _____

as purple as _____

as itchy as _____

as wet as _____

- -

Group's Name _____

Our Analogies

as scared as _____

as little as _____

as purple as _____

as itchy as _____

as wet as _____

Literature-Based Mini-Lessons to Teach Writing   Scholastic Professional Books

Books to Use: Descriptive Language

Brown, M. (1986). *Arthur's Teacher Trouble.* Boston: Little, Brown and Company.

Bunting, E. (1991). *Night Tree.* New York: Harcourt Brace Jovanovich.

Cannon, J. (1993). *Stellaluna.* New York: Harcourt Brace & Company.

Hest, A. (1986). *The Purple Coat.* New York: Macmillan Publishing Company.

Kellogg, S. (1985). *Chicken Little.* New York: Morrow Junior Books.

Meddaugh, S. (1994). *Martha Calling.* Boston: Houghton Mifflin Company.

Nixon, J. (1988). *If You Were a Writer.* New York: Simon & Schuster.

Rylant, C. (1994). *Mr. Putter and Tabby Pour the Tea.* New York: Harcourt Brace & Company.

————— (1985). *The Relatives Came.* New York: Simon & Schuster.

Schwartz, H. (1993). *Backstage With Clawdio.* New York: Alfred A. Knopf, Inc.

Steig, W. (1976). *The Amazing Bone.* New York: Farrar, Straus and Giroux.

Tolhurst, M. (1990). *Somebody and the Three Blairs.* New York: Orchard Books.

Van Allsburg, C. (1985). *The Polar Express.* Boston: Houghton Mifflin Company.

Wells, R. (1991). *Fritz and the Mess Fairy.* New York: Dial Books for Young Readers.

Yolen, J. (1987). *Owl Moon.* New York: Philomel Books.

Young, E. (1992). *Seven Blind Mice.* New York: Philomel Books.

Parts of a Story

CHAPTER 5

The Mini-Lessons

Writing a Complete Story

Exploring Happy Endings

Bringing It All Together—The Ending Sentence

Let's Publish!

The Writing Goals

To write a story with a beginning, a middle, and an ending

To explore possible endings for stories

To write an effective ending sentence

To edit a story for classroom publication

Favorite Books to Use

Stories with easily identified problems and solutions, such as:
Max's Dragon Shirt by Rosemary Wells
Noisy Nora by Rosemary Wells
Sylvester and the Magic Pebble by William Steig

Books with a variety of different endings, such as:
Dr. DeSoto by William Steig
Frederick by Leo Lionni
Jimmy's Boa and the Big Splash Birthday Bash by Trinka Hakes Noble
Just a Dream by Chris Van Allsburg
The Paper Bag Princess by Robert Munsch
The Polar Express by Chris Van Allsburg
Those Summers by Aliki Brandenburg
Three Names by Patricia MacLachlan
The Wump World by Bill Peet

Books with a variety of different ending sentences (in addition to those listed above):
The Art Lesson by Tomie dePaola
Arthur's Teacher Trouble by Marc Brown
Author: A True Story by Helen Lester
The Bookshop Dog by Cynthia Rylant
Harry the Dirty Dog by Gene Zion
My Ol' Man by Patricia Polacco
Owl Moon by Jane Yolen
The Relatives Came by Cynthia Rylant

Writing a Complete Story

GOAL To write a story with a beginning, a middle, and an ending

*T*his year, our introduction to the parts of a story happened at read-aloud time one afternoon. I had just finished reading the part of Sylvester and the Magic Pebble *where Sylvester had turned himself into a rock on* Strawberry Hill. I glanced at my watch and realized our time was up. I closed the book and heard 18 simultaneous "AAAHHHHs." The students responded "But you just can't stop now! What happened to Sylvester?"

Having noticed that many of their stories ended in the middle of the conflict, I said, "Now you know how I feel when you end your stories too soon. You leave me wondering what happened next. Think about Sylvester tonight and what you'd write if you had to help him solve his problem. Tomorrow we'll find out what William Steig decided to write when he ended Sylvester and the Magic Pebble."

The children were delighted the next day when they discovered that Sylvester's problem had been solved with a simple wish. Like many of their stories, the conflict of this story was resolved in less than an instant. Often, following a beginning that leads to a "cliff-hanger" problem, my students resolve their stories with endings similar to the following:

One day I was a little scared. When I was in the woods I was chopping wood. I saw a foot. It was a dinosaur's!!!!!! I ran. I jumped into bed. I was safe.

This impromptu lesson with Sylvester and the Magic Pebble—*or another cliff-hanger story—prompts me to bring another story to our writers' mini-lesson and focus on what makes a complete story.*

BEFORE THE LESSON

I make an overhead transparency of the Story-Parts Sheet at the end of this chapter.

I begin the lesson by reading Noisy Nora, *stopping after "'I'm leaving,' shouted Nora, 'And I'm never coming back!'" I close the book and say, "The End."*

Class:	No! That's not the end!
Mrs. L.:	Sure it is...Didn't you hear me read "The End?"
Dana:	You're just saying that. I know it's not the end because we don't know what happened to Nora.
Mrs. L.:	What do you need to know?
Lauren:	Does Nora run away forever?
Tommy:	We need to know if her parents go to find her.
Stephanie:	It's not a good way to end. It's a sad ending if she never comes back.
Mrs. L.:	Tell me how you would end this story.
Meghan:	I would probably have her parents go find her.
Mrs. L.:	So the audience needs to know what happened next before the story can end. Good writers try not to end a story too soon. Would you like me to finish *Noisy Nora* to find out how Rosemary Wells decided to solve Nora's problem?
Class:	Yes!
	(I read the rest of the story to the class.)
Mrs. L.:	Tell me what you think of this ending.
Stephanie:	It's happy. I like that Nora comes back.
Matthew:	She got some attention from her family too.
Mrs. L.:	Today we are going to decide what makes a complete story. Tell me what you think every story should have.
Carrie:	An ending.
Mrs. L.:	Definitely. What is the first part of a story?
Ryan:	The beginning.
Mrs. L.:	Right. So we write the beginning and then the ending.
Ben:	No, you missed a part.
Mrs. L.:	Which part?
David:	The problem that happens in the story.
Tommy:	That happens before the ending.
Mrs. L.:	Let me see if I have this right. First, you write a beginning.
Class:	Yes.
Rebecca:	That's the once-upon-a-time part.
Ellen:	Where you write about the people in the story and make it exciting.
Mrs. L.:	Okay, then the problem happens next.
Meghan:	That's the middle.
Stephanie:	Then you can write the ending. When the problem is solved.
Mrs. L.:	Great! Let's look at the Story-Parts Sheet and see if we can fill in the blanks using Rosemary Wells' book *Noisy Nora*.

We further explore *Noisy Nora*, discussing the beginning, middle, and ending of the story. As we fill in the sheet, we discuss the importance of each part for making the story complete.

Story-Parts Sheet

Story Title: Noisy Nora   **Author:** Rosemary Wells

Characters: Nora, Mom, Dad, brother Jack, sister Kate

In the Beginning—Meet the characters and the setting

Nora and her family are at home. Nora's parents are busy with Jack and Kate. Nora makes lots of noise. She wants her family to give her some attention.

In the Middle—The problem of the story happens

Nora's family does not notice her but they yell at her for making too much noise. So she leaves. Her family looks for her. They can't find her anywhere. Her family is sad.

At the End—The problem of the story is solved

Nora comes crashing into the room from inside the closet where she was hiding. Her family is happy again.

Extending the Mini-Lesson

OTHER BOOKS

On another day, we try a second Rosemary Wells story, *Max's Dragon Shirt*. Like *Noisy Nora*, this is a rather short story with an easily distinguished problem. I close the book and say "the end" after reading "After a while Max woke up. Ruby was gone..." We agree this is not the ending because we have unanswered questions, so we discuss possible solutions to Max's problem. During the next mini-lesson, I read the rest of the story and we chart the parts of this story on another story sheet.

On subsequent days, perhaps during a readers' workshop lesson, the children are given a story sheet of their own to fill in using a book they've read. They work diligently, exploring the concept of story using the works of expert authors.

READ-ALOUD

After reading aloud stories together, we talk about them and critique their endings. I ask the children to tell me about the beginning, the middle, and the ending. As we discuss various works shared, and as the children continue to look at literature from a writer's perspective, their awareness of the endless possibilities for story endings continues to expand.

TELL ME MORE

As the students work to include suitable endings for the stories they write, our commonly used phrase becomes, "Tell me more." After sharing a story that's not complete, fellow writers automatically ask each other for details about what happened next. The "Tell me more" technique is a great way to elicit more writing from beginning writers. And when the students view providing more details as a game that writers often have to play, they embrace the challenge more enthusiastically.

STORY SHEETS—HELP WITH STORY PLANNING

I make copies of the Story-Parts Sheet (provided at the end of this chapter) available at our writing center. When students are having trouble deciding what should happen next in a story, I help them use a copy to map out a plan. This process helps writers break the parts of the story into concrete pictures and make decisions more easily. I encourage the students, particularly first graders, to use pictures or simple labels to plan the story; otherwise, the job is too time consuming and interest may be lost.

A simple use of a Story-Parts Sheet

A Story Parts Sheet

Story Title: _____

Author: _____ Date: _____

Characters: _____

In the Beginning-- Meet the characters and the setting
Beginning Sentence: _____

In the Middle-- The problem of the story happens

At the End-- The problem of the story is solved
Ending Sentence: _____

Adding an Ending

One morning, Maggie shared her story, "Harry the Handsome Horse," which originally ended with the sentence "I was really sad but I got used to it."

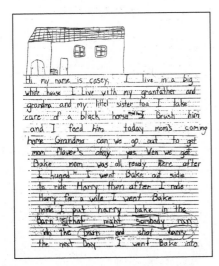

"But your ending left us hanging," one child said. When Maggie's sharing group asked her who shot Harry, she had her writing task for the day. Later that day she read: "We found out who the person was that shot Harry. The police put him back in jail. I wrote in my diary. 'I will always remember you, Harry.'" Short and to the point, this ending satisfied Maggie's audience. Maggie's experience with her sharing group reminded me that:

> The kind of social experience young writers need is to write things however they can, share them with others, and come face to face with their audience's lack of understanding. Then they will be motivated to write in more and more communicative, and hence conventional, ways, especially when they are surrounded by models of more successful communication by professional authors and even by other children.

—The Beginnings of Writing

A writer receives feedback from the audience

Exploring Happy Endings

GOAL To explore possible endings for stories

After the lesson in which we leave Sylvester on Strawberry Hill as a rock, the children begin critiquing the stories we share based on how well the author satisfies their questions at the end. After reading Dr. DeSoto, *a group of students expressed concern about William Steig's ending. "But what will the fox do now that his mouth is glued shut? William Steig didn't tell us!" they complained. We talked about the luxury authors have in choosing whatever ending they wish for a story—as long as most of the questions about the story are answered.*

The solutions continue to be the most difficult part for children to write, especially for first graders. Fletcher explains that:

> ...the writer does not necessarily aim to construct an ending to make the reader gasp (or gag). Rather, the writer tries to marry the right ending for the writing. We can help our students improve their endings by first helping them become aware of the various kinds of endings available to them.
>
> —*What a Writer Needs*

To help build an awareness of possible endings, I share a few of my favorites with the class, including the poetic ending of Frederick, *the unexpected ending of* The Paper Bag Princess, *and Van Allsburg's personal reflection at the end of* The Polar Express. *With these stories in mind, we gather together for a mini-lesson to explore some of our favorite books for endings that are "just right"—and some new ideas of our own.*

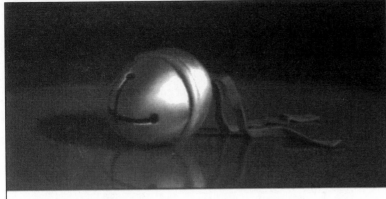

> At one time most of my friends could hear the bell, but as years passed, it fell silent for all of them. Even Sarah found one Christmas that she could no longer hear its sweet sound. Though I've grown old, the bell still rings for me as it does for all who truly believe.

Chris Van Allsburg's ending of The Polar Express

Mrs. L.: As writers, you know that the ending of a story is just as important as the beginning. The beginning needs to grab your audience's attention, but your ending needs to make your audience happy that they read your story. Your ending must also answer most of the questions the reader is asking as he reads your story. Let's look at some of our favorite books to explore the different ways authors have ended their stories. Take a look at the books on the chalk ledge.

(I have written "Story Endings" on the board.)

Ellen: My favorite is *The Paper Bag Princess*.

Mrs. L.: Tell me about that ending.

Ellen: Well, the princess doesn't marry the prince like you would think.

Tommy: But it's still a happy ending because the prince wasn't very nice. The princess saved the prince from the dragon, and he said she looked a mess.

Mrs. L.: So it's a surprise kind of ending but happy, too. I'll write "surprise" as one kind of ending a story may have.

Brett: I like *The Wump World*. It's kind of happy at the end because the wumps get their world back, but it's never the same as it was before the Pollutians destroyed it.

Mrs. L.: I think that ending is the kind that teaches a lesson.

Tommy: Well, you do learn what could happen if we pollute the world.

Brett: So you should write "teach a lesson" on the board.

Mrs. L.: Okay. What about *Three Names* by Patricia MacLachlan? I'll read the last page to refresh your memories:

> ...And Three Names would turn around three times and sigh, settling like a sack of grain beside my great-grandfather, the two of them dreaming away the summer. The two of them waiting for school.

Stephanie: The story could start all over.

Amanda: When the new school year starts.

Mrs. L.:	Good thinking. Maybe I should write "starts all over" as another way to end a story. Can you think of any other stories like that?
Meghan:	What about *Jimmy's Boa*? At the end the kids bring Jimmy as many goldfish as they can buy.
Dana:	And that's how the problem started in the first place—with just one goldfish.
Mrs. L.:	I think that would make *Jimmy's Boa and the Big Splash Birthday Bash* a story that starts all over.
	When a character is remembering something that happened to him or her, it's called a personal reflection. Sometimes, the character is thinking of something that happened to him when he was younger. At the end of *The Polar Express*, the boy is thinking back to the night when he got to choose the first gift of Christmas.
Tommy:	You should write "remembering" on the board too.
Mrs. L.:	Okay, "remembering" or "reflecting" is another kind of ending. Can you find another book in which the character is remembering something that happened years before the story was written?
Stevie:	What about *Those Summers*?
Mrs. L.:	I think so. Aliki writes about "those summers" at the beach with her family when she was a little girl.
Brett:	*Just a Dream* ends with him seeing the trees all grown up, even though he just planted one little tree that morning.
Tommy:	He's dreaming about the trees in the future.
Mrs. L.:	Then *Just a Dream* ends with a personal reflection too. Think about your stories today, and when you get to the ending, decide whether you want to end with a surprise, teach a lesson, reflect on a memory, or have the story start all over again. Remember, you're the author and you can choose to end your story any way you like.

Start all over   Remember or reflect

Story Endings

Surprise   Teach a lesson

Extending the Lesson

MORE BOOKS

Following read-aloud time, we discuss the choice the author made for each story ending. After reading *Arthur's Birthday*, we decide to add "funny" to our list of possible ways to end a story. Our chart begins to look more like a web as we draw lines to connect "funny" to "starts all over," and the children see the connection between several kinds of endings.

WRITE A NEW ENDING

During another mini-lesson, we share a story that is unfamiliar to most of the students. Again, I stop reading just as the adventure reaches its peak of interest. Together, we write our own ending to the story. The next day I read the rest of the story and we discuss the author's choice of an ending.

On subsequent days I read stories from beginning to end and ask, "If you were the author of this story, what ending would you choose?"

MECHANICS: BOOK-SPELLED WORDS

It can be frustrating when words that have been a part of a child's weekly spelling lists don't automatically transfer to story writing efforts. To encourage my students to depend on conventional spelling, or "book-spelling" as we call it, rather than "sound-spelling" (phonetic spelling) for easily spelled, common words, I copy an ending from a favorite book, intentionally misspelling certain words. I proceed to talk about the great ending of the story, ignoring the misspelled words. As with most lessons on mechanics, the students are quick to tell me about my spelling errors, and our mini-lesson then focuses on the book-spelling of some commonly used words. We talk about the need to check stories for spelling during the editing stage. Together, we underline and spell the misspelled words. The following selection is the last page from *Foolish Rabbit's Big Mistake*.

The <u>litl</u> rabbit, still holding the apple, <u>hopt</u> back to the <u>trea</u>. He lay <u>don</u> beneath the branches, sighed contentedly, and took a big <u>bit</u> <u>ov</u> the apple. And <u>thet's</u> the end of the <u>store</u>.

Sound-Spelling	Book-Spelling
litl	little
hopt	hopped
trea	tree
don	down
bit	bite
ov	of
thet's	that's
store	story

Adding a Twist at the End

Allie combined her love of dinosaurs and Cynthia Rylant's book *The Relatives Came* in her story called "When the Dinosaurs Left." Allie included all the necessary components of a story and added an extra twist with her ending that "starts all over": "Then we got in the car and took Fred home. Sam felt like hitting himself. Then he met our new neighbors. Dun-Du-Dun-Dunt." Allie's story was created out of "images, characters, actions, and themes that come from the literature she has heard, as well as from her family life." *(The Beginnings of Writing).*

When the dinosaurs left!

Wen the dinosaurs left every one was sad aspeshtily Sam He I dont wat every one to go looder and looded He was so mad it hert every ones ecsel He was sent to his room but he did not stop!! It was time to sasey gedby then sam and his cusins fred took a stuft dinosaur and put it in freds plase in the wagincar. Then hid under the bed freds family left and Fred was stil ther. Sam snuk out and got some cookys. Then desurd under the

bed. Then Sam and Fred ate and ate intil they were stuft with cookys. I was looking for Sam I looked and I looked and I looked?!! but I cold not finde Sam If I didnd mother wood not like it. So I cept on looking BuT then it was diner time I had to do someing. I went to mom She said were is sam? I said he is cleaning his room ok that was the only reason mom wood let us mis diner She asked "cen I see hoow cleen it is?" um um

um nanna "wy not?" Becae" becae wy "he wants to be ulon" then out pept sam and fred and rane to mom. Mother gave the rast of the potados. Then we got in the car and took fred haume. Sam felt like hiting him seth then he met are noow naber dun dududdui.
The End

Allie: "When the Dinosaurs Left"

Bringing It All Together— The Ending Sentence

GOAL To write an effective ending sentence

Writing complete stories is not something that magically happens to beginning writers. In fact, taking your time is crucial. You need to take time to build trust, time to build confidence, and time to encourage risk-taking. Most important, beginning writers need time to feel successful. Often they share "finished" first drafts only to have their fellow writers send them back for more writing in order to answer questions the audience may have.

Usually, the children's first step in completing a story is to erase the words "The End." Beginning writers love to write those words. It gives closure to their great efforts and usually signals the teacher, "I'm done, so don't ask me to write one more word on this particular piece of paper." I've discovered that when I ask students in the early stages of writing development—often my first graders—to tell me "what happened next," they will verbally rattle off what would amount to another page of writing. But my suggestion to write one more sentence causes them to remind me, "I'm finished" and point to the words "The End."

So, I collect some of our favorite books, and we meet during a mini-lesson to look at the endings of these stories again. We find the exact place where the story could have ended, where most of the questions about the story have been answered. Then we read on and discover that many expert writers have a clever way of bringing all of the ideas of the story together with one extraordinary or often rather simple ending sentence.

Mrs. L.: I know you enjoyed *Dr. De Soto* by William Steig, and some of us especially liked the ending where Dr. and Mrs. De Soto "outfox the fox" by gluing his mouth shut. Did you know that William Steig actually wrote an extra page? He could have ended his story after the fox left "with dignity." This is where the problem is solved.

Stevie: Because the fox leaves without eating them.

Mrs. L.:	Right. But on the last page he wrote: "Doctor De Soto and his assistant had outfoxed the fox. They kissed each other and took the rest of the day off." Tell me what you think about these extra words.
Meghan:	They make the ending more detailed.
Mrs. L.:	I agree, and these words make the ending special. I bet when William Steig wrote them he felt they were "just right."
Katie:	Maybe he imagined how happy they were—so happy they kissed.
Mrs. L.:	Adding extra words means writing a little more to bring the story to a close in a fun or special way. I picked a few other favorite books. Let's see how some of our other favorite books ended.
	Here's *The Polar Express*. This story could have ended…
Ben:	…when he opened the package with the bell inside.
Mrs. L.:	Right. But Chris Van Allsburg added an extra page: "At one time most of my friends could hear the bell, but as years passed, it fell silent for all of them. Even Sarah found one Christmas that she could no longer hear its sweet sound. Though I've grown old, the bell still rings for me as it does for all who truly believe."
Ben:	I believe!
Lauren:	Me too. That's good for people who don't believe to read.
Mrs. L.:	Every time I read those words, I think they are "just right." And I like how that extra page takes us into the future when the children are older.
	You all laughed when I read the last page of *Arthur's Teacher Trouble*.
Mrs. L.:	I think the story could have ended when Mr. Ratburn said he was very proud of Arthur. Then Marc Brown added, "But next year I look forward to a new challenge…Teaching Kindergarten." Are you glad Marc Brown added this last page?
Matthew:	I think the last page makes the book even better.
Stephanie:	Because then we know what's going to happen next.
Brett:	Yeah, D.W. gets to have "The Rat."
Mrs. L.:	How about *Owl Moon*?
Meghan:	It ends when they see the owl.
Mrs. L.:	Well, actually that's the part when the problem is solved. But Jane Yolen adds a last page: "When you go owling you don't need words or warm or anything but hope. That's what Pa says. The kind of hope that flies on silent wings under a shining Owl Moon."
Ellen:	That's pretty.
Mrs. L.:	Yes, it is. I bet Jane Yolen had to work extra hard to think of these words. She didn't give up when she solved the problem. She added some words to bring the story to a close. I think a writer knows when to end the story.
Matthew:	Maybe it's just when you think it's over, then you try to add a little bit more.

Mrs. L.:	Could be. Tomie dePaola added just four words to his story *The Art Lesson* to bring it to a close and help us see what happened in the future. Do you remember when the problem is solved?
Amanda:	When he gets to draw his own picture.
Sara:	After he did what the teacher said.
Mrs. L.:	Right. Tomie dePaola wrote "And he did" under the picture of the turkey and pilgrims. Then he wrote it again under his picture of the art teacher. But there's a last page that says, "And he still does."
Carrie:	Because he still draws pictures.
Brett:	So we know this is a true story about Tomie dePaola.
Mrs. L.:	Yes. I'm glad he wrote this extra sentence. It tells us more about the story and shows Tomie dePaola as an adult, sitting at his desk, drawing.
Tommy:	Look, even his hair is kind of gray.
Mrs. L.:	That's a great picture clue, isn't it? Patricia Polacco writes an ending that makes you think of the future too—or what happens now that she's grown up—in *My Ol' Man*.

...Anytime I want, I get quiet and still inside, and I am little again. I think of that summer by Potter's Pond. I have the gift of that memory anytime I recall it. A memory that brings back Gramma, the parrots, the cruising machine, and, most especially, my ol' man. A memory that will last as long as children tell others about fathers they love.

Meghan:	That makes you feel like you feel when you remember a good memory.
Carrie:	I like that feeling.
Mrs. L.:	Me too. Did you remember that the first part of that sentence is at the beginning of the story too? "Whenever I get quiet and still inside and wish I was little again..." This page brings the beginning and the ending together. Sometimes, it helps to go back to the beginning of your story and try to think of a way to connect it with the ending of your story.
	Let's look at another favorite book, *The Relatives Came*. It has a kind of "warms your heart" ending too.
Samuel:	It ends when they drive home.
Ryan:	Something about going to bed.
Stephanie:	And missing the relatives.
Mrs. L.:	The last page is extra but closes the story in a special way. Cynthia Rylant wrote: "And when they were finally home in Virginia, they crawled into their silent, soft beds and dreamed about next summer."
Ben:	That lets you know there's more to the story.
Ellen:	The story repeats next summer.
Mrs. L.:	It makes it a happy ending, doesn't it? We know they are sad because they miss each other, so they dream about the next time they'll be together. I like that.

Amanda: Me, too.

Mrs. L.: *Harry the Dirty Dog* has a special ending sentence.

Ben: Harry is clean again?

Mrs. L.: Remember the sneaky thing Harry does? Here's the last page:

> It was wonderful to be home. After dinner, Harry fell asleep in his favorite place, happily dreaming of how much fun it had been getting dirty. He slept so soundly, he didn't even feel the scrubbing brush he'd hidden under his pillow.

Tommy: If that sentence hadn't been there, we wouldn't know about the brush.

Brett: I like that sentence. It's funny.

Lauren: It's just right!

Mrs. L.: Here's another dog book, *The Bookshop Dog*. Do you remember the last sentence?

David: Something about Martha Jane the dog going to Hawaii.

Mrs. L.: Right. Cynthia Rylant wrote, "She loved Hawaii!"

Matthew: And just three little words made our whole class laugh.

Mrs. L.: So it's definitely worth the extra effort for that ending sentence. Today when you're searching for those words that you know will make your story "just right," think a little bit harder before you write the words "The End." Think about your story and think of words that will give the reader just a little more information—a hint about something that might happen next or to connect something you wrote earlier in the story to the ending.

Extending the Lesson

OUR ENDING SENTENCES

Just as we did for beginning sentences, we chart favorite ending sentences from the authors of children's literature. I begin to record good endings from student writing and create an Excellent Story Endings chart. The children are often surprised to see the products of their fellow writers who worked hard and wrote sentences as detailed as those of the experts. Sometimes I mix the children's endings in with the experts' endings for an even more dramatic effect.

When the party was over, I washed my clown face off, returned my outfit, and went home. The End.

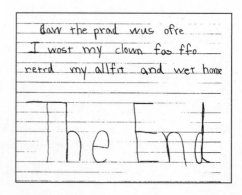

Favorite Story Endings

- They kissed each other and took the rest of the day off. (Dr. De Soto)

- Though I've grown old, the bell still rings for me as it does for all who truly believe. (The Polar Express)

- "...But next year I look forward to a new challenge...Teaching kindergarten." (Arthur's Teacher Trouble)

- The kind of hope that flies on silent wings under a shining Owl Moon. (Owl Moon)

- And he still does. (The Art Lesson)

- A memory that will last as long as children tell others about fathers they love. (My Ol' Man)

- And when they were finally home in Virginia, they crawled into their silent, soft beds and dreamed about next summer. (The Relatives Came)

- He slept so soundly, he didn't even feel the scrubbing brush he'd hidden under his pillow. (Harry the Dirty Dog)

- She loved Hawaii. (The Bookshop Dog)

Some Excellent Story Endings

- He broke the piñata at the birthday party. It was the best birthday party ever! (Joe)
- ...and that was the end of that! (Tommy)
- ...it hit the ground with a big BOOM and was never seen again. (Stephanie)
- The dog jumped into the warm bed as it snowed outside. (Maddie)
- The next morning I had four quarters in the bag I put my tooth in. What will I spend it on? (Tracie)
- Mammals are amazing animals! (John)

FOR HOMEWORK

After our lesson on ending sentences, I assign an "at-home" project. At the beginning of the week, I ask the students to copy the following note:

Bring a book from home with a favorite ending sentence.

Each day, we take time for students to share their selected books and sentences. We discuss what it is that makes these sentences our "favorites" and how effectively these sentences end a particular story.

This extension activity could be used for any writers' workshop goal and provides an opportunity to share the learning process with parents.

The Writing Conference

"THE END"

From this time forward, we have a vocabulary for discussing our stories. If a student's story is missing a component, it's either the "beginning," the "problem," or the "solution" to the problem. I remember reading in *The Beginnings of Writing* that a teacher's "job as writing coach is to discern the structure inherent in the story the child is writing and talking about, and to ask questions that help the child make it clear to the reader" (p.166). Our discussions following read-aloud time and writing mini-lessons help the students focus on the structure of the experts' stories. The focus during our writing conference is the structure of their own writing efforts.

For our writing conference on parts of a story, I photocopy the Story-Parts Sheet (provided at the end of this chapter) for each child. After a student shares a story with me, I fill in the parts of the Story Sheet, using the child's ideas. I also record the student's beginning and ending sentence. Seeing the story broken into parts helps us focus on the beginning, middle, and ending of a story and helps to guide our conference.

Tommy's Conference

Mrs. L.: Tommy, what story are we sharing today?

Tommy: "The Wild Crazy Ride."

Mrs. L.: Great title! Is this a true story?

Tommy: Kind of...it's based on a ride I went on. But I've never been to Six Flags.

Mrs. L.: Please read your story.

Tommy: Today my dad, me and mom went to Six Flags and went on the roller coaster and got dizzy. And all of a sudden we spinned and clanked and rolled. And then the ride was over.

Mrs. L.:   I like the words "spinned and clanked and rolled." Those are great describing words. Let's put your story on a Story Sheet to make sure you've got all of the main parts.

Tommy: Well, I have a title, and I know I'm the author!

Mrs. L.:   Yes, that's a good start. Let me fill in your beginning sentence: "Today my dad and me and mom went to Six Flags and went on the roller coasters and got dizzy." So going on the roller coasters at Six Flags is your beginning.

Tommy: My middle is that we spinned and clanked and rolled. And my ending is when the ride was over.

Mrs. L.:   You know, I'm curious about what you were thinking as you were spinning and clanking and rolling. Could you tell me that part?

Tommy: Well, it felt like we just started spinning and then it was over.

Mrs. L.:   So you felt like it ended too quickly, and you were disappointed?

Tommy: No, I was nervous, and I was glad when it was over.

Mrs. L.:   Let's try to put that sentence in the story.

Tommy: How about if I write "I was nervous. I was glad when the ride was over" after "we spinned and clanked."

Mrs. L.:   Sounds great to me. Now you have a problem to be solved.

Tommy: I think I'll add, "I was very scared."

Mrs. L.:   Great thinking. Can you think of another sentence to add at the end—to show that your story may start over or give a personal reflection.

Tommy: You mean add more words to make it "just right"?

Mrs. L.:   Sure. I'm wondering what happened when the ride was over.

Tommy: I ran and got back in line for the roller coaster again.

Mrs. L.: I think you should tell your audience that you got back in line.

Tommy: Then my story starts all over.

Mrs. L.: That's a great way to end your story.

Tommy: Maybe I could say, "Dad, can we go on that ride again?"

Mrs. L.: I think you've got a complete story that starts over again.

Tommy: And again, and again.

Story-Parts Sheet from Tommy's conference

> **A Story Parts Sheet**
>
> **Story Title:** The Wild Crazy Ride
>
> **Author:** Tommy   **Date:** Oct. 14
>
> **Characters:** Mom, Dad, Tommy
>
> **In the Beginning—** Meet the characters and the setting
> **Beginning Sentence:** Today my Dad and me and Mom went to Six Flags.
>
> They go on the roller coaster.
>
> **In the Middle—** The problem of the story happens
> Tommy is nervous and very scared.
> They spin, clank and roll.
>
> **At the End—** The problem of the story is solved
> **Ending Sentence:** "Dad, can we go on that ride again?"
>
> The ride ends. Tommy wants to try the roller coaster again!

GREATEST ACCOMPLISHMENTS IN WRITING

To help monitor student progress, I also use a Greatest Accomplishments in Writing sheet (provided at the end of this chapter) that includes samples of story leads and descriptive language, as well as titles of completed stories. This sheet is helpful to share with parents when discussing student progress in writing.

Discussing a student's progress with her parent.

Nicky's Mystery Writing

Many of the stories the children write require several weeks of writers' workshop time. For children like Nicky, who didn't always feel successful with reading, writing had become a time to look forward to every day. By the time Nicky had finished writing "Stormy Night," he was eager to share his accomplishment with the class and ready to move on to a new topic. His story was well received by his classmates, many of whom decided to give mystery writing a try. The look of pride on Nicky's face as he shared his story was one of the highlights of my year.

Nicky: "Stormy Night"

It was a stormy night. I was out on the docks. A steamy fog blew by. A cold hand fell on my shoulder. I turned around. I saw nothing. I stepped a little closer. I fell into a hole. I saw two eyes. The two eyes wrestled me. The monster punched me. He dragged me upstairs. Police were there. The police arrested him. The police gave him bread and water. I got hurt more than you think. I'm in the hospital. But I'm glad that monster is in jail.

Let's Publish!

GOAL To edit a story for classroom publication

Helen Lester's book, Author: A True Story, *which I discovered at a children's literature conference, gave me the idea for a great writer's workshop mini-lesson. I knew my beginning writers would love the comical way Helen Lester describes the struggles all authors face. She explains how, when a book is finally in print, the triumphs make up for all the disappointments in a writer's life and that becoming an author is "better than a dream come true." Anxious to share this author's true story with my students, I went straight to the bookstore, bought my own copy, and began marking the pages with sticky notes. I used the book to introduce a mini-lesson on publishing your own story. Publishing a favorite story to share with classmates allows the children to experience the steps a "real" author must go through—from formulating an idea to working with an "editor." Our mini-lesson went something like this:*

Mrs. L.: I discovered a new book this weekend, and I can't wait to share it with you.

Tommy: Is it about a dog?

Mrs. L.: No, but there's a picture of a dog in the story. It's about another of my favorite things—writing. It's called *Author: A True Story.* It's written by Helen Lester.

Brett: I wonder why the cover shows a person behind a shower curtain holding some paper.

Meghan: I bet she's trying to write a story in the shower!

Ryan: If it's a true story, then her paper got wet!

Mrs. L.: Let's read to find out the true story about this author.

(We read the story together.)

Mrs. L.: Tell me what you think about this true story.

Stephanie: I felt sorry for her whenever she said there wasn't a line to have people sign her books, but the line to the famous author was long.

Tommy: But she said that was the first time she signed books. I bet she has a long line now.

Matthew: I thought it was funny when she was writing on her sock because she didn't have any paper with her when she thought of her idea.

Sara:	I know how she feels about not being able to find a title. That's the hard part.
Joe:	I can't find my pencil sometimes.
Mrs. L.:	Things like this happen to all authors, I guess.
Meghan:	I like that feeling when you can't write fast enough.
Mrs. L.:	That's the page when she's writing on her sock. Here it is—page 24: "I love it best when ideas are hatching so fast I can barely write them down." I like to think of ideas as hatching. I also like the 'Fizzle Box' idea on the next page. But I especially liked her ending page: "I'm glad I didn't join the circus. Even though writing is hard work, it's what I love to do. I never dreamed I'd become an author. So this is better than a dream come true."
Tracie:	I want to be an author when I grow up.
Others:	Me too.
Mrs. L.:	Why wait? You've all written some exciting stories that you should be proud of. I'm sure you could "publish" a book for our classroom.
Amanda:	How?
Mrs. L.:	We could make books to share with one another, books of the favorite stories we've written.
Colleen:	We'd need an editor.
Matthew:	I'll do it!
Meghan:	No, Mrs. L. should be the editor. She's good at giving us ideas.
Sara:	And she knows when a word needs to be fixed up.
Mrs. L.:	I'd be happy to be your editor.
John:	We also need a "typer." Sometimes my printing is hard to read.
Mrs. L.:	I'll bet some parents would be happy to type our stories on the computer for you to illustrate. First, let's make a list of what we should do to get ready to publish a story.
Brett:	Well, first we have to have a great idea.
Kristen:	To be a published story, it probably should be the kind of story that you don't want to stop writing when writers' workshop is over.
Mrs. L.:	Good thinking. Tell me what this great story must have.
Tommy:	It has to have a beginning, a middle, and an ending.
Mrs. L.:	I'll add this to our list.
Alissa:	The beginning should make the audience want to read more.
John:	The story should paint pictures with words too.
Matthew:	It should have a good ending sentence too.
Mrs. L.:	I agree. This is a lot for a writer to remember. I guess that's why authors have to work so hard. So when you think you've written one of those extra-special stories, with words that paint pictures, an exciting beginning and ending, and all the main parts included, what should happen next?
David:	The writer should share the story with someone.

Matthew:	To see if anything is missing.
Mrs. L.:	Okay. What happens next?
Meghan:	Usually, there are changes to be made. I had to erase the words "The End" yesterday to add an exciting sentence.
Mrs. L.:	Helen Lester said she keeps looking for ways to improve her story until it's time for her story to be printed. The editor may ask for certain changes too.
Meghan:	Doesn't the writer make the story look almost perfect before sending it to the editor?
Mrs. L.:	I think that sounds like a good idea. So you make changes with a friend, give the story to the editor, then make more changes if the editor says so.
Stephanie:	When the story is just right, it's printed. The writer knows when the story is just right.
Mrs. L.:	I agree. Tell me what happens next.
Colleen:	After it's printed, the story needs to be illustrated.
Mrs. L.:	Is that the end of the publishing process?
Tracie:	What about the dedication?
Joe:	And the fancy cover?
Brett:	Sometimes there's a page that tells about the author too. Like *The Bookshop Dog* shows Cynthia Rylant with her dog, Martha Jane.
Mrs. L.:	Right. Let's call these extra things—the dedication, author page, and cover—the finishing touches.
Tommy:	This might take a long time.
Tracie:	But it'll be fun.
Mrs. L.:	Smile if you think seeing your book in print "might be better than a dream come true."
	I see from your smiles, that we're ready to open Room Four's Publishing Shop.

Extending the Mini-Lesson

PUBLISHING CENTER

After our mini-lesson on publishing, I read the story *How a Book Is Made*, which gives young writers a behind-the-scenes tour of the book making process. The story depicts the people involved in making a book—from the author and illustrator team to the publisher and the printer. (This is also a great book to share before taking a field trip to a library or bookstore.)

When one of my students has worked carefully to complete an "extra-special" story, he or she gets the chance to "publish" it, after editing it with me. I make a How to Publish a Story chart and hang it at the Writing Center. Students refer to this chart to be sure they've included all the essential elements in their favorite story. By leaving out a step, they risk rejection from the editor!

How to Publish a Story

1. Think of a great idea.

2. Use this idea to write a really great story.

3. Make sure the story has:

   - a great beginning.
   - words that paint pictures.
   - a beginning, a middle, and an ending.
   - an ending sentence that brings the story together.

4. Read the story with a friend.

5. Make changes.

6. Share the story with the editor.

7. Make more changes.

8. When the story is just right, the editor has the story typed.

9. Illustrate the story.

10. Add the finishing touches:

    - a fancy cover.
    - a dedication page.
    - an about-the-author page.

I rely on parent volunteers to input each story on the computer using "book-spelling." We format the story like a picture book, allowing space at the top of each page for illustrations. Over the next several days, the student uses "special" erasable crayons or watercolor paints to illustrate the book. To make the book look even more professional, we add an about-the-author page, a dedication page, and a wallpaper cover. I make sure each student has one specially "published" story for the year. This activity is particularly motivating for those students who often have difficulty writing a story from beginning to end or who lose interest in a story before they complete it.

A published story.

ABOUT-THE-AUTHOR PAGES

As part of the finishing touches on the students' published books, each child completes the about-the-author page, which tells of hobbies, family members, favorite adventures, and other information particularly relevant to the story in the book. I introduce this as a mini-lesson during which we share book jackets featuring some favorite authors. Cynthia Rylant's *The Bookshop Dog*, Vera Williams's *A Chair for My Mother*, Ed Young's *Seven Blind Mice*, and Jane Yolen's *Owl Moon* offer a variety of ways authors choose to share information about themselves. *Hog Eye* by Susan Meddaugh is an example of how an author used her sense of humor to provide biographical information.

> This Writer is a Stodot at F.T.
> and a god riter on Childnring
> Books. And ih his fre time he
> woks his dog. And Som of
> the Books he as Ritn is, Star
> Stor WArS Book.
> Batmah and Aobih.
> The Pot of god ahd, So math mon.

Sample first graders' About-the-Author pages

This writer is a student at F. T. and a good writer of children's books. And in his free time he walks his dog. And some of the books he has written are Star War books, Batman books, The Pot of Gold and so much more.

> She goes to Ferguson twp. school.
> She has a very friendly teacher that always
> has a smile on her face. She loves to play ball
> with her dog. She has to birds. She loves
> to watch funny movies. She likes to read and write
> none she has time. She loves to swimme alot.

A rough copy of an About-the-Author page before it was typed and printed

FIZZLE BOX

In *Author: A True Story*, Helen Lester describes her Fizzle Box as "A whole box full of fizzled thoughts and half-finished books. Whenever I need an idea, I can go to the box and find wonderful things—just the name I needed! A funny word! A wise lesson!"

Our class Fizzle Box includes the same such items—unfinished stories, favorite words that paint pictures, analogies, tired-word replacements. When a young writer thinks of a writing-related tip, it is included in our class Fizzle Box, so that others may borrow a thought when they need it most. The box has no particular organization strategy, but young authors happily peruse it without complaint.

AN AUTHORS' TEA

A special way to celebrate a year of great writing effort is to have an "Authors' Tea." The students design invitations during writers' workshop, inviting their parents, grandparents, or a special friend to school for a writing celebration. During the next several writers' workshop periods, we practice reading our selected stories using a microphone (or our best read-aloud voices). On the day of the Authors' Tea, the children, often dressed in their "Sunday best," take turns sharing their published stories before enjoying juice and cookies with their parents.

An author prepares a book for the Authors' Tea.

A Classful of Confident Writers

The evidence that I needed to show the success of one year's writing process and the effect of saturating a classroom with quality literature can be seen in my students' progress. Besides feeling confident in their writing efforts, the students, without exception, grow in their ability to communicate as writers. Whether it's going from all illustrations to two sentences of text, or developing a style and cadence of literature, the progress is apparent. The quality of their stories and their enthusiasm and pride in completed drafts make writers' workshop time rewarding for everyone.

Take Molly, for example. This first grader went from writing short, repetitive stories to writing one story that she worked on for over a month.

Molly, Beginning of First Grade

Sound-spelling and reading came easily for Molly. Her difficulty was with finding topics to write about that held her interest. A week before she wrote "Sylvester's First Day of School," I made a note to myself about Molly's writing progress. I noticed that she'd reached a plateau, was having difficulty finding topics, and seemed unenthusiastic at writers' workshop time. So I allowed Molly to spend her writers' workshop period at the Favorite Books center. She'd always been enthusiastic about read-aloud time, racing to get a front-row center seat.

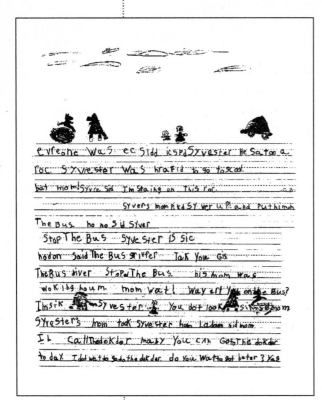

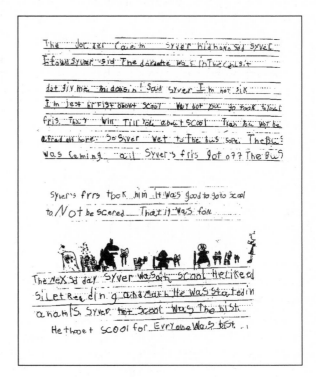

Molly, End of First Grade

Everyone was excited except Sylvester. He sat on a rock. Sylvester was horrified to go to school. "But Mom," Sylvester said, "I'm staying on this rock." Sylvester's mom picked Sylvester up and put him on the bus. "Oh, no," said Sylvester. "Stop the bus. Sylvester is sick." "Hold on," said the bus driver. "Thanks you guys." The bus driver stopped the bus. His mom was walking home. "Mom, wait!" "Why aren't you on the bus?" "I'm sick," said Sylvester. "You don't look sick," said Mom. Sylvester's mom took Sylvester home. "Lay down," said mom, "I'll call the doctor. Maybe you can go to the doctor today." "I don't want to go to the doctor." "Do you want to get better?" "Yes." The doctor came. Sylvester hid. "Oh, no," said Sylvester. "I found Sylvester," said the doctor. "He was in the closet." "Don't give me any medicine!" said Sylvester, "I'm not sick.

I'm just nervous about school." "Why don't you talk to your friends. They will tell you about school. Then you won't be afraid any more." So Sylvester went to the bus stop. The bus was coming. All Sylvester's friends got off the bus. Sylvester's friends told him it was good to go to school, to not be scared, that it was fun. The next day Sylvester was at school. He liked silent reading and math. He was studying about animals. Sylvester thought school was the best. He thought school for everyone was best.

Molly's progress is a reminder that writing takes time, that it is a developmental process no adult can rush. Although it seemed as though Molly's transformation from early writer to superior writer happened overnight, she had actually spent an entire school year researching the world of literature and making discoveries as a process writer. Her sentence variety and use of conversation and story structure, as well as her vocabulary, blossomed with exposure to and enthusiasm for literature.

Students who have participated in literature-based mini-lessons have an advantage over those in a traditional writers' workshop. They leave the transitional stage between early and confident writer, armed with a style they have learned from the "experts." At read-aloud time they listen with a writers' perspective, absorbing the experts' tricks of the trade without realizing it. Listening to a story for the simple joy it provides is a worthwhile activity for all children. Focusing instruction on that same story in a mini-lesson gives young writers time to practice using hints from the experts.

After four years of developing literature-driven mini-lessons, my hopes for the beginning writers in my classes have become a reality. I've done my best to encourage their potential, praise their efforts, and immerse them in an environment of quality children's literature. I've helped them look to the experts with a writer's eye. My reward is knowing I've helped nurture a group of confident writers who demonstrate a growing awareness of language, an appreciation for literature, and a love of writing.

The success of literature-based mini-lessons is evident not only in the students' writing products but in their excitement about writing and literature. Their books, marked with sticky notes, line the chalk ledge. Their stories, attached to clipboards, are carried outside for recess. Their pleas for five more minutes of writing time make my heart skip a beat. As my students continue to discover what it is they like about the stories they read, hear, or write, they continue to help me make decisions about our next mini-lesson based on children's literature. Now, when the students meet me on the carpet for a mini-lesson, I smile instead of panic, confident that the authors of children's literature will add a little magic and, most important, that these beginning writers will write happily ever after.

Name _____

 # Story Parts Sheet

Story Title: _____

Author: _____ Date: _____

Characters: _____

....

In the Beginning — Meet the characters and the setting

Beginning Sentence: _____

....

In the Middle — The problem of the story happens

....

At the End — The problem of the story is solved

Ending Sentence: _____

Name _____

My Greatest Accomplishments in Writing

Sample Story Leads

Date

_____ 1. _____

_____ 2. _____

_____ 3. _____

_____ 4. _____

_____ 5. _____

Samples of Descriptive Language

Date

_____ 1. _____

_____ 2. _____

_____ 3. _____

_____ 4. _____

_____ 5. _____

Titles of Complete Stories

Date

_____ 1. _____

_____ 2. _____

_____ 3. _____

_____ 4. _____

_____ 5. _____

Additional Comments on Back

Books to Use: Parts of a Story

Brandenberg, A. (1986). *How a Book Is Made.* New York: Harper & Row Publishers.

———— (1996). *Those Summers.* New York: HarperCollins Publishers.

Brown, M. (1989). *Arthur's Birthday.* Boston: Little, Brown and Company.

———— (1986). *Arthur's Teacher Trouble.* Boston: Little, Brown and Company.

dePaola, T. (1989). *The Art Lesson.* New York: G. P. Putnam's Sons.

Lionni, L. (1967). *Frederick.* New York: Alfred A. Knopf.

Maclachlan, P. (1991). *Three Names.* New York: HarperCollins Publishers.

Martin, R. (1985). *Foolish Rabbit's Big Mistake.* New York: G. P. Putnam's Sons

Munsch, R. (1980). *The Paper Bag Princess.* Toronto: Annick Press Ltd.

Noble, T. (1989). *Jimmy's Boa and the Big Splash Birthday Bash.* New York: Dial Books for Young Readers.

Peet, B. (1970). *The Wump World.* Boston: Houghton Mifflin Company.

Polacco, P. (1995). *My Ol' Man.* New York: Philomel Books.

Rylant, C. (1996). *The Bookshop Dog.* New York: Blue Sky Press.

———— (1985). *The Relatives Came.* New York: Aladdin Books.

Steig, W. (1982). *Dr. De Soto.* New York: Farrar, Straus and Giroux.

———— (1969). *Sylvester and the Magic Pebble.* New York: Simon & Schuster, Inc.

Van Allsburg, C. (1990). *Just a Dream.* Boston: Houghton Mifflin Company.

———— (1985). *The Polar Express.* Boston: Houghton Mifflin Company.

Wells, R. (1991). *Max's Dragon Shirt.* New York: Dial Books for Young Readers.

———— (1973). *Noisy Nora.* New York: Dial Books for Young Readers.

Williams, V. (1982). *A Chair for My Mother.* New York: Greenwillow Books.

Yolen, J. (1987). *Owl Moon.* New York: Philomel Books.

Zion, G. (1956). *Harry the Dirty Dog.* New York: Harper & Row Publishers.

Book Lists

C H A P T E R **6**

Comprehensive List of Books Used Throughout the Mini-Lessons

Babbitt, N. (1994). *Bub or the Very Best Thing*. New York: HarperCollins Publishers.

Bang, M. (1994). *One Fall Day*. New York: Greenwillow Books.

Brandenberg, A. (1986). *How a Book Is Made*. New York: Harper & Row Publishers.

——— (1996). *Those Summers*. New York: HarperCollins Publishers.

Brett, J. (1991). *Berlioz the Bear*. New York: G. P. Putnam's Sons.

——— (1987). *Goldilocks and the Three Bears*. New York: G. P. Putnam's Sons.

Brown, M. (1992). *Arthur Babysits*. Boston: Little, Brown and Company.

——— (1989). *Arthur's Birthday*. Boston: Little, Brown and Company.

——— (1986). *Arthur's Teacher Trouble*. Boston: Little, Brown and Company.

——— (1996). *Arthur Writes a Story*. New York: Little, Brown and Company.

Bunting, E. (1991). *Night Tree*. New York: Harcourt Brace Jovanovich.

Calhoun, M. (1991). *High-Wire Henry*. New York: Morrow Junior Books.

Cannon, J. (1993). *Stellaluna*. New York: Harcourt Brace & Company.

Carle, E. (1969). *The Very Hungry Caterpillar*. New York: Philomel Books.

Catalanotto, P. (1995). *The Painter*. New York: Orchard Books.

Cummings, P. (1992). *Talking With Artists*. New York: Bradbury Press.

dePaola, T. (1989). *The Art Lesson*. New York: G. P. Putnam's Sons.

Ehlert, L. (1990). *Feathers for Lunch*. Orlando, Fl: Harcourt Brace Jovanovich.

Guarino, D. (1989). *Is Your Mama a Llama?* New York: Scholastic Inc.

Henkes, K. (1991). *Chrysanthemum*. New York: Greenwillow Books.

Hest, A. (1984). *The Crack of Dawn Walkers*. New York: Macmillan Publishing Company.

——— (1993). *Nana's Birthday Party*. New York: Morrow Junior Books.

——— (1986). *The Purple Coat*. New York: Macmillan Publishing Company.

Houston, G. (1992). *My Great-Aunt Arizona*. New York: HarperCollins Publishers.

Ingman, B. (1995). *When Martha's Away*. Boston: Houghton Mifflin Company.

Isaacs, A. (1994). *Swamp Angel*. New York: Bantam Doubleday Dell Publishing Group, Inc.

Johnson, A. (1993). *Julius*. New York: Orchard Books.

Kaye, M. (1990). *The Real Tooth Fairy*. New York: Harcourt Brace & Company.

Kellogg, S. (1985). *Chicken Little*. New York: Morrow Junior Books.

———— (1986). *Best Friends*. New York: Dial Books for Young Readers.

———— (1996). *Yankee Doodle*. New York: Aladdin Paperbacks.

Kovacs, D., Preller, J. (1991). *Meet the Authors and Illustrators: Volume One*. New York: Scholastic, Inc.

———— (1993). *Meet the Authors and Illustrators: Volume Two*. New York: Scholastic, Inc.

Kraus, R. (1971). *Leo the Late Bloomer*. New York: Harper and Row.

Lester, H. (1997). *Author: A True Story*. Boston: Houghton Mifflin Company.

Lionni, L. (1967). *Frederick*. New York: Alfred A. Knopf.

Maclachlan, P. (1991). *Three Names*. New York: HarperCollins Publishers.

Martin, R. (1985). *Foolish Rabbit's Big Mistake*. New York: G. P. Putnam's Sons

Mckissack, P. (1988). *Mirandy and Brother Wind*. New York: Bradbury Press.

Meddaugh, S. (1994). *Martha Calling*. Boston: Houghton Mifflin Company.

———— (1995). *Hog Eye*. Boston: Houghton Mifflin Company.

Munsch, R. (1980). *The Paper Bag Princess*. Toronto: Annick Press Ltd.

Nixon, J. (1995). *If You Were a Writer*. New York: Simon & Schuster.

Noble, T. (1989). *Jimmy's Boa and the Big Splash Birthday Bash*. New York: Dial Books for Young Readers.

Peet, B. (1970). *The Wump World*. Boston: Houghton Mifflin Company.

Pilkey, D. (1993). *Dogzilla*. New York: Harcourt Brace & Company.

Polacco, P. (1993). *Babushka Baba Yaga*. New York: Philomel Books.

———— (1995). *My Ol' Man*. New York: Philomel Books.

———— (1994). *My Rotten Redheaded Older Brother*. New York: Simon & Schuster.

Rylant, C. (1996). *The Bookshop Dog*. New York: Blue Sky Press.

———— (1985). *The Relatives Came*. New York: Simon & Schuster.

———— (1994). *Mr. Putter and Tabby Pour the Tea*. New York: Harcourt Brace & Company.

———— (1982). *When I Was Young in the Mountains*. New York: E. P. Dutton.

Schwartz, H. (1993). *Backstage With Clawdio*. New York: Alfred A. Knopf, Inc.

Scieszka, J. (1991). *The Frog Prince Continued*. New York: Penguin Books.

———— (1989). *The True Story of the Three Little Pigs*. New York: Penguin Books.

Sendak, M. (1963). *Where the Wild Things Are*. New York: Harper and Row.

Speed, T. (1995). *Two Cool Cows*. New York: G. P. Putnam's Sons.

Steig, W. (1976). *The Amazing Bone*. New York: Farrar, Straus and Giroux.

———— (1982). *Dr. De Soto*. New York: Farrar, Straus and Giroux.

———— (1969). *Sylvester and the Magic Pebble*. New York: Simon & Schuster.

Tolhurst, M. (1990). *Somebody and the Three Blairs*. New York: Orchard Books.

Van Allsburg, C. (1990). *Just a Dream*. Boston: Houghton Mifflin Company.

———— (1985). *The Polar Express*. Boston: Houghton Mifflin Company.

Waber, B. (1987). *Funny, Funny Lyle*. Boston: Houghton Mifflin Company.

Weller, F. (1990). *Riptide*. New York: The Putnam & Grosset Group.

Wells, R. (1991). *Fritz and the Mess Fairy*. New York: Dial Books for Young Readers.

———— (1991). *Max's Dragon Shirt*. New York: Dial Books for Young Readers.

———— (1973). *Noisy Nora*. New York: Dial Books for Young Readers.

Wilson, G. (1994). *Prowlpuss*. Cambridge: Candlewick Press.

Wolff, P. (1995). *The Toll-Bridge Troll*. New York: Harcourt Brace & Company.

Yolen, J. (1987). *Owl Moon*. New York: Philomel Books.

Young, E. (1992). *Seven Blind Mice*. New York: Philomel Books.

Zion, G. (1965). *Harry the Dirty Dog*. New York: Harper and Row.

References

Atwell, N. (1987). *In the Middle: Writing, Reading and Learning With Adolescents*. Portsmouth, NH: Heinemann.

Calkins, L. M. (1986). *The Art of Teaching Writing*. Portsmouth, NH: Heinemann.

Fletcher, R. (1993). *What a Writer Needs*. Portsmouth, NH: Heinemann.

Temple, C., Nathan, R., Temple, F., & Burris, N. A. (1993). *The Beginnings of Writing* (3rd Ed.). Boston: Allyn and Bacon.

The Favorite Books Box

More Recommended Books for a Literature-Based Writers' Workshop:

BOOKS THAT HELP WITH GETTING THE WORKSHOP STARTED

Ackerman, K. (1988). *Song and Dance Man*. New York: Alfred A. Knopf.

Brown, M. (1994). *Arthur's First Sleepover*. New York: Little, Brown and Company.

Ehlert, L. (1993). *Nuts to You.* New York: Harcourt Brace Jovanovich.

Finchler, J. (1995). *Miss Malarkey Doesn't Live in Room 10.* New York: Walker and Company.

Flournoy, V. (1985). *The Patchwork Quilt.* New York: Dial Books for Young Readers.

Henkes, K. (1996). *Lilly's Purple Plastic Purse.* New York: Greenwillow Books.

Hopkins, L. (1990). *Good Books, Good Times!* New York: HarperCollins Publishers.

Little, J., Devries, M. (1991). *Once Upon a Golden Apple.* New York: Viking.

Polacco, P. (1994). *Firetalking (Meet the Author).* New York: Richard C. Owen Publishers, Inc.

Pulver, R. (1991). *The Holiday Handwriting School.* New York: Macmillan Publishing Company.

Wells, R. (1973). *Benjamin and Tulip.* New York: Random House.

Books That Help with Exploring Story Leads

dePaola, T. (1982). *Strega Nona's Magic Lessons.* New York: Harcourt Brace Jovanovich.

Kellogg, S. (1983). *Ralph's Secret Weapon.* New York: E. P. Dutton, Inc.

Lionni, L. (1992). *Mr. McMouse.* New York: Alfred A. Knopf.

Munsch, R. (1992). *Purple Red and Yellow.* New York: Annick Press.

Peet, B. (1978). *Eli.* Boston: Houghton Mifflin Company.

Pilkey, D. (1993). *Kat Kong.* New York: Harcourt Brace & Company.

Polacco, P. (1992). *Picnic at Mudsock Meadow.* New York: G. P. Putnam's Sons.

Schwartz, D. (1985). *How Much Is a Million?* New York: Lothrop, Lee & Shepard Books.

Waber, B. (1974). *Lyle Finds His Mother.* New York: Houghton Mifflin Company.

Williams, V. (1986), *Cherries and Cherry Pits.* New York: Greenwillow Books.

———— (1990). *More More More Said the Baby.* New York: Greenwillow Books.

Books That Help With Descriptive Language

Bang, M. (1983). *Dawn.* New York: William Morrow and Company, Inc.

Hirschi, R. (1991). *Harvest Song.* New York: Cobblehill Books.

Huck, C. (1989). *Princess Furball.* New York: Greenwillow Books.

Polacco, P. (1992). *Mrs. Katz and Tush.* New York: Dell Publishing.

———— (1991). *Some Birthday.* New York: Simon & Schuster.

Rylant, C. (1988). *All I See.* New York: Orchard Books.

Schwartz, A. (1982). *Bea and Mr. Jones.* New York: Bradbury Press.

Van Allsburg, C. (1981). *Jumanji.* New York: Houghton Mifflin Company.

Wells, R. (1989). *Max's Chocolate Chicken.* New York: Dial Books for Young Readers.

Williams, V. (1982). *A Chair for My Mother.* New York: Greenwillow Books.

Yolen, J. (1987). *Piggins.* New York: Harcourt Brace Jovanovich.

BOOKS THAT HELP WITH PARTS OF A STORY

Cooney, N. (1989). *The Umbrella Day.* New York: Philomel Books.

dePaola, T. (1993). *Tom.* New York: G. P. Putnam's Sons.

Henkes, K. (1993). *Owen.* New York; Greenwillow Books.

Johnston, T. (1992). *Lorenzo the Naughty Parrot.* New York: Harcourt Brace Jovanovich.

Karlin, B. (1989) *Cinderella.* Boston: Little, Brown and Company.

Kirk, D. (1994). *Miss Spider's Tea Party.* New York: Scholastic Inc.

Lindbergh, R. (1990). *The Day the Goose Got Loose.* New York: Dial Books for Young Readers.

Pilkey, D. (1994). *Dog Breath.* New York: Blue Sky Press.

Polacco, P. (1990). *Thundercake.* New York: Philomel Books.

Scieszka, J. (1992). *The Stinky Cheese Man and Other Fairly Stupid Tales.* New York: Penguin Books.

Yorinks, A. (1986). *Hey, Al.* New York: Farrar, Straus and Giroux.

Additional Teacher Resources

Kemper, D., Nathan, R., Sebranek, P. (1996) *Write Away.* Wilmington, MA: Great Source Education Group, Inc.

Meet the Author Books. New York: Richard C. Owen Publishers, Inc.

Routman, R. (1991). *Invitations: Changing as Teachers and Learners K–12.* Portsmouth, NH: Heinemann.

Wells, J., Hart-Hewins, L. (1994). *Phonics, Too! How to Teach Skills in a Balanced Language Program.* Ontario: Pembroke Publishers.